# Reasons
*to* **Believe**

A Survey of Christian Evidences

# Reasons *to* Believe

## A Survey of Christian Evidences

Chad Ramsey

Gospel Advocate Company
Nashville, Tennessee

Published by Gospel Advocate Co.
1006 Elm Hill Pike, Nashville, TN 37210
http://www.gospeladvocate.com

ISBN-10: 0-89225-561-7

ISBN-13: 978-0-89225-561-0

# Dedication

To Beverly, the love of my life.

And to Johnson, Anna Mae and Jake Franklin,
whose faith I pray will be strengthened
by the words of this book.

# Table of Contents

# Introduction

There is no denying that we live in an age in which many individuals are skeptical of religion in general, and of Christianity in particular. Some of this skepticism has resulted from the hypocritical behavior of those who claim to follow Christ. When individuals hear Christians saying one thing but doing another, they conclude that the message of Christianity is either unimportant or irrelevant. Either way, the message loses its appeal and skepticism results. This could be avoided if every Christian would heed the admonition of Jesus: "Let your light so shine before men, that they may see your good works and glorify your Father in heaven" (Matthew 5:16).

Another factor contributing to religious skepticism is the mistaken idea that matters of religion are based upon faith, whereas matters of science are based upon fact. Those who advocate this distinction speak and write as if modern science and its discoveries stand in complete contradiction to belief in God or in the Bible. Nothing could be further from the truth! The very definition of biblical faith, "Now faith is the substance of things hoped for, the evidence of things not seen" (Hebrews 11:1), clearly asserts the relationship of faith to evidence. Rather than being baseless, faith is based firmly upon the reality of God and His word (Romans 10:17).

Nevertheless, individuals act as if religion and reason are incompatible. Because of this, men and women have avoided studying arguments for God's existence, the deity of Christ, and the inspiration of the Bible. So instead of developing the kind of faith that moved Peter to say: "Lord, to whom shall we go? You have the words of eternal life. Also we have come to believe and know that You are the Christ, the Son of the living God" (John 6:68-69), many individuals have come to doubt that Christians are able to defend their beliefs against the attacks of atheism and agnosticism.

This book was written to combat doubt. In fact, it is the contention of this book that evidence is available to support the conclusion that God exists, that Jesus of Nazareth is the Son of God, and that the Bible is the inspired word of God. A careful examination of this evidence will strengthen the believer and challenge the unbeliever. My hope and prayer are that the one who reads this book will give fair consideration to the evidence that is presented, and that upon considering the evidence, he or she will emerge with both a stronger faith and a stronger resolve to do the will of God. Truly, Christians have reasons to believe!

## Chapter 1

# Why Study Christian Evidences?

Before we begin any serious examination of a subject, it is helpful to know what one might hope to gain from engaging in that study. Thus, we would do well to ask: Why should we study Christian evidences?

## Is Evidence Really Necessary?

As we seek to answer the question, "Why should we study Christian evidences?" it should be noted that there are some who posit that Christians should not seek evidence to support their religious beliefs. They say that the pursuit of evidence actually diminishes the faith of the individual. One who argued this was the philosopher Søren Kierkegaard (1813-1855). Kierkegaard is perhaps best known for describing faith as a "leap in the dark." He wrote:

> Without risk there is no faith. Faith is precisely the contradiction between the infinite passion of the individual's inwardness and the objective uncertainty. If I am capable of grasping God objectively, I do not believe, but precisely because I cannot do this I must believe. If I wish to preserve myself in faith I must constantly be intent upon holding fast the objective uncertainty, so that in the objective

uncertainty I am out "upon the seventy thousand fathoms of water," and yet believe. [1]

Kierkegaard's idea could be summarized in two ways: (1) Faith is a reaction, based upon one's feelings, to what is unknown. (2) Faith is not the result of knowledge but rather a belief without basis. Accordingly, if one tried to provide grounds for his belief, he would remove the very thing that made faith what it is – a trusting response despite the unknown.

Although Kierkegaard does not do so in this passage, those who hold to his position often cite 2 Corinthians 5:7 to prove this point: "For we walk by faith, not by sight." Ironically, instead of proving the position of the one who takes faith to be a blind leap into the dark, Paul's admonition does just the opposite. Within its context, the passage is instructing those who face physical difficulties to seek faithfully the place where no sorrow or pain exists – heaven. And Paul is powerfully illustrating that although we cannot see heaven in a physical sense, we can know that it is real by faith. Heaven is unseen, but it is certainly not unknown.

A number of key passages could be cited from Scripture to show that Kierkegaard's approach to faith is invalid. First, we could show from Hebrews 11 that faith, rather than being a response to the unknown, is actually a response to the command of God. What motivated Noah to build the ark (v. 7)? It was the same thing that caused Abraham to offer his son Isaac as a sacrifice (v. 17) – faith. Because we know from consulting Scripture that Noah did not build the ark on a whim (Genesis 6:13-22) and that Abraham did not simply decide on his own to offer Isaac as a sacrifice before he received God's command (22:1-2), we can rightly conclude that faith is a response to the command of God. No wonder Paul wrote: "So then faith comes by hearing, and hearing by the word of God" (Romans 10:17).

Second, we could show from John 20:30-31 that the very purpose of John's gospel account was to provide a reason for individuals to believe in Jesus. He wrote: "And truly Jesus did many other signs in the presence of His disciples, which are not written in this book; but these are written that you may believe that Jesus is the Christ, the Son of God, and that believing you may have life in His name." If it is true that we can come to believe in Jesus by considering the works He performed while on earth, it is true that our belief is based upon evidence and not the lack thereof.

Additionally, we could strengthen this case by noting some of the arguments that Peter used when he preached to the Jews on Pentecost (Acts 2:14-39). In the midst of his sermon, Peter presented at least two arguments in hopes of convincing the Jews of Jesus' identity. He argued: (1) The Jews could have known who Jesus was by considering His works (v. 22). (2) The tomb of David was occupied while the tomb of Jesus was empty (vv. 29-32). If faith, as Kierkegaard supposes, is based upon what is "objectively uncertain," Peter's factual arguments make no sense. Nevertheless, Peter did use arguments to appeal to the Jews. Thus, we may rightly conclude that faith is not based upon the uncertain but rather upon the certain.

But what does a discussion of faith have to do with studying Christian evidences? Primarily, it shows that faith requires evidence. Because we cannot please God without faith (Hebrews 11:6), we should all want to have an adequate foundation upon which to base our beliefs.

## Three Good Reasons to Study Christian Evidences

(1) We should study Christian evidences so that our faith can be strengthened. Just as the apostles requested: "Increase our faith" (Luke 17:5), we should seek to grow in our faith as well. In fact, the faith of a Christian ought to be of such a nature that he or she can respond like Peter, who said to Jesus: "Lord, to whom shall we go? You have the words of eternal life. Also we have come to believe and know that You are the Christ, the Son of the living God" (John 6:68-69). Rather than thinking that God's existence is probable, the Christian must know that God exists. Rather than thinking that Jesus likely is the Son of God, the Christian must know. And rather than considering that Scripture possibly contains God's message, the Christian must have no doubt that the Bible is the result of divine inspiration.

(2) We should study Christian evidences to determine what is true. The Bible does not discourage the search for evidence. In fact, it admonishes us to "[t]est all things; hold fast what is good" (1 Thessalonians 5:21). Rather than shying away from an examination of the arguments for or against God's existence, the deity of Christ, and the in-

spiration of Scripture, the Christian must remember that the truth sets men free (John 8:32). Because truth has no reason to fear, those who search for truth ought not to fear the results of their quest.

(3) We should study Christian evidences so that we can teach others. As Peter wrote, we must "always be ready to give a defense to everyone who asks [us] a reason for the hope that is in [us], with meekness and fear" (1 Peter 3:15). If we do not know why we believe what we believe, it is likely that we really don't believe anything at all.

## Examining the Evidence

If Scripture does anything, it appeals to men to consider the appropriate evidence. That is why Paul "reasoned with [the Thessalonians] from the Scriptures, explaining and demonstrating that the Christ had to suffer and rise again from the dead, and saying, 'This Jesus whom I preach to you is the Christ' " (Acts 17:2-3). And that is why John described Jesus as: "That which was from the beginning, which we have heard, which we have seen with our eyes, which we have looked upon, and our hands have handled, concerning the Word of life" (1 John 1:1). Truly, the evidence to support Christianity is available and it begs to be examined.

## Questions for Consideration

1. Why would an individual argue that faith needs no evidence?

2. How might you respond to this and support your answer with Scripture?

3. Does 2 Corinthians 5:7 support the idea that faith is a "leap into the dark"? Why or why not?

4. What can be gained by studying the evidences supporting Christianity?

## Chapter 2

# God's Existence: From Cause to Design

At some time, you may have pondered the question of whether God exists. If so, you probably did what men usually do when searching for truth – you considered the available evidence.

But before an examination of any theistic arguments, it should be noted that God's existence does not depend upon man's ability to present arguments in His favor. Whether I have the ability to convince a single reader that God exists does not establish or diminish the truth of the matter. "If a theistic argument is rejected, an assurance in God's existence and ability to save has not been dealt a fatal blow. God does not rely upon theistic argumentation to convince people of the gospel." [1]

Because the evidence for God's existence is commonly presented in argument form, whether you knew it at the time, you probably thought about the question of God's existence in light of a particular argument. For example, if you concluded that God must exist because the world exists, you used what is known as the cosmological argument. Or if you concluded that God must exist because the intricate details of the world point to an intelligent designer, you followed the teleological argument. These are not the only two arguments presented in hopes of proving God's existence. Others will also be considered, but the cosmological and teleological arguments are widely used.

Nevertheless, Scripture, although it does not present specific arguments for God's existence, presupposes God's existence, and emphasizes the necessity of believing He exists. As Hebrews 11:6 states: "But without faith it is impossible to please Him, for he who comes to God must believe that He is, and that He is a rewarder of those who diligently seek Him." Thus, in hope of strengthening our belief in God's existence, we now turn our attention to the arguments commonly used.

## The Cosmological Argument

The cosmological argument, also known as the causal argument for God's existence, is based upon the relationship between cause and effect. Like most of the other arguments we will study, it reasons from the existence of the world to the existence of God. Because of this, it is called an a posteriori argument – an argument based upon experiences or things that can be experienced with the senses.

The cosmological argument is actually found within Scripture. For example, when the psalmist wrote: "The heavens declare the glory of God; and the firmament shows His handiwork" (Psalm 19:1), he was arguing that man could reason from the existence of the world to the realization of a glorious God. Likewise, when Paul rebuked the Roman Gentiles for their ignorance of God's existence and power (Romans 1:18-21), he did so in view of what they could have known had they examined the world and reasoned correctly about it.

Although the roots of the cosmological argument can be traced to the ancient Greeks, it was made prominent by the Catholic philosopher Thomas Aquinas (1225-1274). In his work, *Summa Theologica*, Aquinas wrote: "The existence of God can be proved in five ways." [2] Interestingly, of the five ways he presented, the first three are variations of the cosmological argument:

> The first and more manifest way is the argument from motion. It is certain, and evident to our senses, that in the world some things are in motion. Now whatever is moved is moved by another, for nothing can be moved except it is in potentiality to that towards which it is moved; whereas a thing moves inasmuch as it is in act. For motion is nothing else than the reduction of something from potentiality to actuality. But nothing can be reduced from potentiality to ac-

tuality, except by something in a state of actuality... .
Therefore, whatever is moved must be moved by another.
... But this cannot go on to infinity, because then there would
be no first mover, and, consequently, no other mover, seeing that subsequent movers move only inasmuch as they are
moved by the first mover ... .

The second way is from the nature of efficient cause. In the
world of sensible things we find there is an order of efficient causes. There is no case known (neither is it, indeed,
possible) in which a thing is found to be the efficient cause
of itself; for so it would be prior to itself, which is impossible ... . Now to take away the cause is to take away the effect. ...

The third way is taken from possibility and necessity, and
runs thus. We find in nature things that are possible to be
and not to be ... . But it is impossible for these always to
exist, for that which can not-be at some time is not.
Therefore, if everything can not-be, then at one time there
was nothing in existence. Now if this were true, even now
there would be nothing in existence, because that which does
not exist begins to exist only through something already existing ... . Therefore we cannot but admit the existence of
some being having of itself its own necessity, and not re-
ceiving it from another, but rather causing in others their necessity. This all men speak of as God.[3]

For the sake of brevity, we could sum up all of what Aquinas said by
simply stating that every effect must have an adequate cause. If the
world is the effect, then it must owe its origin to something other than
itself. Therefore, the adequate cause of the world must be God. In argument form, it might look something like this:
(1) There are things that come into existence.
(2) These things owe their origin to other things (they are contingent be-
    ings).
(3) Contingent beings are finite by virtue of their nature.
(4) A finite being cannot have infinite existence.
(5) Therefore, because there are things that exist, there must be an ul-

timate, non-contingent cause for their existence.

(6) The cause of all things must be God.

To make matters clear, consider the following examination of the cosmological argument in light of Hebrews 3:4: "For every house is built by someone, but He who built all things is God." In this passage, the house is obviously contingent. Had its builder decided not to build it, it would not exist. But just as the house is contingent upon its builder, the builder is also a contingent being. Had his parents not met, he would never have been born and thus never built the house. The same thing, of course, could be said about his parents, and so on. But the series cannot regress into infinity because contingent beings (such as the builder and his parents) are finite. That is why Hebrews 3:4 affirms so confidently, "He who built all things is God." There must be a first cause, and God is the first cause.

## The Teleological Argument

Like the cosmological argument, the teleological argument is based upon experience. In particular, it claims to find an intelligent purpose in the way that our world is constructed. This design, the argument goes, can be seen in both the universe in general and in the human body particularly. With regard to the human body, the argument could aptly be applied to any of the intricate systems of which it is composed. For example, who would argue that man's respiratory system lacks design? Or that the circulatory system lacks purpose?

With this in mind, the writer of Proverbs confidently affirmed: "The hearing ear and the seeing eye, the Lord has made them both" (20:12). The text does not merely say that God made the ear and the eye; it emphasizes that God made the ear so that it could hear and the eye so that it could see. The function of the ear and eye were part of God's ultimate plan.

Using the design of the human eye to make the teleological argument, James D. Bales, in the *Bales-Teller Debate*, remarked:

> Let us now consider the eye. It was by the use of the intelligence of man, and the use of the eye, that man constructed the telescope. But the eye is remarkable beyond any comparison with a telescope, which after all is a product of intelligence. The eye is a growth, but not in the sense that the

telescope is, since the eye is an organ and not a material machine. The mind behind the eye translates the impressions which we receive into vision. Thus, we see things, not vibrations. Nothing would be seen with the telescope if the eye, with a mind behind it, was not looking through the telescope. The eye can change from a microscope, so to speak, into a telescope several times within a minute without our being conscious of the adjustment of the mechanism. It has a self-acting mechanism which enables it to clean itself. It has a mechanism for constant repair, up to a certain point, of course.[4]

He concluded: "It is inconceivable that so complex an optical instrument (it is more than that, of course) as the eye could be created or improved by pure chance." No wonder the psalmist penned, "I will praise You, for I am fearfully and wonderfully made; marvelous are Your works, and that my soul knows very well" (Psalm 139:14).

When applied to the universe, the teleological argument is no less impressive. Describing the earth as being "fine-tuned for life," the argument asserts that the world exists in exactly the right circumstances to make life possible. Quoting A.C. Morrison, Bales also made use of this branch of the argument:

We have found that the world is in the right place, that the crust is adjusted to within ten feet, and that if the ocean were a few feet deeper we would have no oxygen or vegetation. We have found that the earth rotates in twenty-four hours and that were this revolution delayed life would be impossible. If the speed of the earth around the sun were increased or decreased materially, the history of life, if any, would be entirely different. We find that the sun is the one among thousands, which could make the sort of life possible on earth, its size, density, temperature, and the character of its rays all must be right, and are right. We find that the gasses of the atmosphere are adjusted to each other and that a very slight change would be fatal.[5]

Aquinas' fifth way to prove God's existence is based upon the design present within the world:

The fifth way is taken from the governance of the world. We see that things which lack knowledge, such as natural bodies, act for an end, and this is evident from their acting always, or nearly always in the same way, so as to obtain the best result. Hence, it is plain that they achieve their end, not fortuitously, but designedly ... [6]

The thesis of the teleological argument is actually quite simple: the existence of intelligent design necessitates the existence of an intelligent designer. The argument could be constructed in this manner:
(1) If the world exhibits intelligent design, there must be an intelligent designer.
(2) The world does show signs of intelligent design.
(3) Therefore, an intelligent designer – God – exists.

When questions such as, "Where did the world come from?" or "Why does the world look like it was designed?" are asked, the cosmological and teleological arguments prove to be quite valuable. The cosmological argument adequately answers the first question by confidently asserting that God is ultimately the cause of all things. The teleological argument answers the second question by identifying God as the intelligent designer. Both arguments provide strong evidence for individuals to believe in the existence of God.

## Questions for Consideration
1. What does the term "a posteriori" mean?

2. Why are the cosmological and teleological arguments called "a posteriori" arguments?

3. What is the basis for the cosmological argument?

4. Do you believe the arguments used by Thomas Aquinas strengthen the cosmological argument? Why or why not?

5. Discuss Hebrews 3:4 as it applies to the cosmological argument.

6. What is the basis for the teleological argument?

7. What particular areas best illustrate the teleological argument?

8. Discuss Proverbs 20:12 as it applies to the teleological argument.

## Chapter 3

# God's Existence: From Being to Morality

Having introduced what are perhaps the two most common arguments used to prove God's existence – the cosmological and teleological arguments, we now direct our attention to two other arguments that are sometimes presented. The first of these, the ontological argument, is found most commonly in philosophical works. Because of its complexity, it is rarely used, but it is worthy of our consideration. The second argument presented in this chapter, the moral argument, is considered by some, including me, to be the most powerful of all the arguments for God's existence. That does not mean that the other arguments lack validity. It does, however, mean that the moral argument can be used to present evidence for God's existence in a very convincing way. Therefore, any study of God's existence would be incomplete without a consideration of these two important arguments.

## The Ontological Argument

Compared to other arguments used to prove God's existence, the ontological argument is certainly unique. Whereas most arguments are structured so that one begins by considering a sensory experience and concludes that God must exist, the ontological argument does just the opposite. Rather than beginning with what is known by means of the senses, the argument begins by considering the concept of God apart from any experience. For this reason, the ontological argument is an a priori argument – an argument based upon knowledge attained either independently or prior to experience. Because the word "ontological" refers to being or existence, the argument could correctly be described as an argument for God's existence based upon the very concept of God's existence.

The ontological argument was first set forth by Anselm of Canterbury (1033-1109). Describing God, Anselm wrote: "You are something than which nothing greater can be thought." [1] After establishing that God is the greatest conceivable being, Anselm went on to argue that if there is a greatest conceivable being, that being must exist not only in mind but also in reality.

> Even the Fool, then, is forced to agree that something-than-which-nothing-greater-can-be-thought exists in the mind, since he understands this when he hears it, and whatever is understood is in the mind. And surely that-than-which-a-greater-cannot-be-thought cannot exist in mind alone. For if it exists solely in the mind, it can be thought to exist in reality also, which is greater. If then that-than-which-a-greater-cannot-be-thought exists in the mind alone, this same that-than-which-a-greater-cannot-be-thought is that-than-which-a-greater-can-be-thought. But this is obviously impossible. Therefore there is absolutely no doubt that something-than-which-a-greater-cannot-be-thought exists both in the mind and in reality. [2]

A summary of Anselm's argument might look something like this:

(1) I have in my mind an idea of the greatest conceivable being.

(2) I can conceive of the greatest conceivable being existing not only in my mind but also in reality.

(3) To exist in both my mind and reality is greater than to exist in my mind alone.

(4) Therefore, the greatest conceivable being must exist in both my mind and in reality.

As you might expect, the ontological argument, which is actually presented in a number of different ways, has been met with a great deal of criticism. One such criticism was offered by Gaunilo, a contemporary of Anselm. In a response titled, "On Behalf of the Fool," Gaunilo applied Anselm's reasoning "to things other than God, things which we know don't exist." [3] Seeking to show the ontological argument to be absurd, he tried to use its approach to prove the existence of the greatest conceivable island. And while this might seem like a powerful objection, to be fair to Anselm, it should be noted that not everyone thinks Gaunilo's criticism is valid. William L. Rowe wrote:

> In defense of Anselm against Gaunilo's objection, we should note that the objection supposes that Gaunilo's island is a possible thing. But this requires us to believe that some finite, limited thing (an island) might have unlimited perfections. And it is not at all clear that this is possible. [4]

Whether this or any criticism leveled against the ontological argument results in its dismissal is certainly debatable. What is clear is that the argument seems to stand or fall with the question of whether existence is an attribute in the same way power and knowledge are attributes. If so, the argument has merit; if not, it must either be revised or abandoned.

## The Moral Argument

The moral argument for God's existence is based upon the idea that right and wrong exist in an objective sense. This implies that there is a standard which is clearly recognized by most people. [5] Such a standard, of course, could not be the product of men because other men would have liberty to change it if they wished, thereby making it subjective. Instead, the standard to which all men are accountable must necessarily transcend humanity. Thus, the thesis of the moral argument is that the existence of objective law necessitates the existence of an objective lawgiver. That lawgiver, of course, is God.

Hastings Rashdall explains effectively why objective rules can come only from God and not from some other source:

> An absolute Moral Law or moral idea cannot exist in material things. And it does not (as we have seen) exist in the mind of this or that individual. Only if we believe in the existence of a Mind for which the true moral ideal is already in some sense real, a Mind which is the source of whatever is true in our own moral judgments, can we rationally

think of the moral idea as no less real than the world itself. Only so can we believe in an absolute standard of right and wrong, which is as independent of this or that man's actual ideas and actual desires as the facts of material nature. The belief in God, though not (like the belief in a real and active self) a postulate of there being any such thing as Morality at all, is the logical presupposition of an "objective" or absolute Morality. A moral ideal can exist nowhere and nohow but in a mind; an absolute moral ideal can exist only in a Mind from which all reality is derived. Our moral ideal can only claim objective validity in so far as it can rationally be regarded as the revelation of a moral ideal eternally existing in the mind of God. [6]

With that being said, two other facts must be considered. First, although all men do not acknowledge the existence of an objective law in word, most men live as if they acknowledge this law. C.S. Lewis recognized this practice and pointed out that men show it to be true when they quarrel. He wrote, "Quarreling means trying to show that the other man is wrong. And there would be no sense in trying to do that unless you and he had some sort of agreement as to what Right and Wrong are." [7] Similarly, H.P. Owen observed:

If moral judgments are merely expressions (or descriptions) of approval it is impossible to understand how they can become the cause of rational disagreement. If I like tea and my friend likes coffee I do not attempt to convert him. But if I hear someone commending the conduct of a rogue I consider his opinion dangerously wrong. Clearly I am justified in condemning someone else's moral judgment only if I can give reasons for my condemnation. It is the absence of any reasons for my preference for tea which makes it absurd for me to challenge my friend's preference for coffee. In other words, if my moral preferences are to be rational, they must be based upon criteria of an objective kind. [8]

We could add that men seemingly do not want to live in a society that lacks objective rules. As Lewis noted: "Human beings, after all, have some sense; they see that you cannot have real safety or happiness except in a society where everyone plays fair, and it is because they see this that they try to behave decently." [9] Significantly, neither atheists nor theists want to live in a world where men are free to determine for themselves (by virtue of their own self-governing ability) if they will rape or refrain from raping.

A second fact that must likewise be considered is that whether men do what they should, their behavior does nothing to discredit the existence of an objective moral law. For men's actions to be weighed in the balances and found lacking, there must be a standard to which they are compared. And if it is granted that one's behavior can improve, we must, of necessity, have a way whereby we can judge this improvement. Lewis also recognized this fact:

> Progress means not just changing, but changing for the better ... . The moment you say that one set of moral ideas can be better than another, you are, in fact, measuring them both by a standard, saying that one of them conforms to that standard more nearly than the other. But the standard that measures two things is something different from either. You are, in fact, comparing them both with some Real Morality, admitting that there is such a thing as Right, independent of what people think, and that some people's ideas get near to that real Right than others. [10]

To summarize the moral argument, consider the following syllogism presented by Thomas B. Warren in the *Warren-Flew Debate*:

> If the moral code and/or actions of any individual or society can properly be subjects of criticism (as to real moral wrong), then there must be some objective standard (some "higher law which transcends the provincial & transient") which is other than the particular moral code which has an obligatory character which can be recognized.

> The moral code and/or actions of any individual or society can properly be subjects of criticism (as to real moral wrong).

> Therefore, there must be some objective standard (some "higher law which transcends the provincial and transient") which is other than the particular moral code and which has obligatory character which can be recognized. [11]

The next logical step is to argue that such a standard must have a source. That source, of course, is God. Why is it wrong to murder, or why is it wrong to rape? Are those actions wrong simply because of the decree of man? Are they wrong without explanation? Or are they wrong because of the decree of God? The moral argument holds the latter and, in so doing, makes a strong case for the existence of an objective lawgiver.

The ontological and moral arguments approach the question of God's existence from unique perspectives. The former focuses upon the very concept of existence and asserts that existence is a necessary attribute of the greatest conceivable being – God. The latter considers objective ideals that are commonly recognized and inquires about their source. If it is wrong to murder or rape, the moral argument asks: why are those actions wrong? It then contends that the existence of objective law implies the existence of an objective lawgiver. That lawgiver, of course, must be God.

## Questions for Consideration

1. Why is the ontological argument considered an a priori argument?

2. What did Anselm mean when he argued that God was the "greatest conceivable being"?

3. Discuss Gaunilo's objection to Anselm's version of the ontological argument? Does it have merit?

4. How would you evaluate the ontological argument? Do you believe that it can be used to prove God's existence?

5. What is the basis for the moral argument?

6. What does "objective" mean?

7. What can be inferred from the fact that men's actions are subject to evaluation?

8. Discuss the possible sources for objectivity.

9. How would you evaluate the moral argument? Do you believe that it can be used to prove God's existence?

10. Discuss the existence of the conscience and how it supports the moral argument.

## Chapter 4

# God's Existence: From the Resurrection to Divine Revelation

The final arguments considering God's existence that we will examine are both based upon God's interaction with the world. The first, commonly referred to as the argument from religious experience, is often presented in a manner that is not subject to verification. If presented in this way, the argument is difficult to support. We will look at ways to present it so that it can be verified. The other argument that will be considered in this chapter is based upon the existence of the Bible. It contends that the Bible is a book that could not be produced by mere men. If, of course, that claim is true, then it must also be true that God exists.

## The Argument From Religious Experience

The argument from religious experience claims that one can know that God exists because of a personal experience that has transpired in his or her own life. Admittedly, the basis of this argument – if one has an experience that defies natural explanation, it implies the existence of a supernatural power – has some merit. Nevertheless, we must be quick to recognize that not every experience an individual has can be counted as genuine. This fact must be considered when one examines the argument from religious experience. As A.E. Taylor says, "All experience is liable to misinterpretation." Because of this principle, Taylor continued, "We may readily admit, then, that much which the experiencer is inclined to take for 'religious' experience is illusion." [1]

But does the fact that men experience illusions or dreams negate the possibility of one having a genuine religious experience? Taylor did not think so:

> We must not argue that sense-perception does not reveal a world of really existing bodies, which are no illusions of our imagination, on the ground that there are such things as dreams and hallucinations, any more than we may argue from the general reality of things perceived by sense to the reality of dream-figures or ghosts. So again we may neither argue that there is no real beauty in the visible world because the best of us are capable of finding it where it is not, nor that because there is real beauty, every supposed beauty detected by any man must be real. [2]

To be fair, we should note that the argument from religious experience has at least one glaring error: how does one distinguish between the contradictory claims made by individuals or groups? For example, Joseph Smith (1805-1844), founder of the Mormonism, claimed that he received a message from the angel Moroni. Similarly, Muhammad (570-632) claimed to have received a message from Gabriel which was eventually written as part of the Koran. Because the messages written by Smith and Muhammad stand in direct opposition to one another, they cannot both be true. Without sufficient reasons upon which to base our acceptance of either individual's claim, both claims must also be dismissed. Thus, the argument from religious experience suffers greatly because it is often presented in a purely subjective manner. Because of this fact, A.E. Taylor correctly observed that "there is no line of argument that lends itself more readily to abuse." [3]

With that being said, to dismiss the argument from religious experience totally would be to go too far. This is especially true when one considers that Christianity is based upon Jesus leaving heaven and coming to the earth, living, dying and being resurrected from the dead. Because numerous events are recorded in Scripture that, if authenticated, imply the existence of God, the argument could be modified and stated in the following manner:

(1) If even one event has taken place that defies natural law or a natural explanation, that event must have resulted by virtue of a supernatural power – i.e., God.

(2) One event has taken place that defies natural law or a natural explanation – the resurrection of Jesus.

(3) Therefore, the resurrection of Jesus must have resulted by virtue of a supernatural power.

(4) Therefore, God exists.

Having thus transformed the argument from religious experience from a subjective argument based upon the accounts of individuals to an objective argument based upon the resurrection, we must now consider whether Jesus actually rose from the grave. If He did, the above version of the argument from religious experience can be used to prove God's existence; if He did not, at the very least, the entire system of Christianity must be set aside.

The significance of the question of whether Jesus was resurrected is obvious. Concerning this question, J.W. McGarvey wrote, "If Jesus arose from the dead, the other miracles will be admitted, as well as all else that is claimed for Jesus in the New Testament." [4] We could add that if Jesus arose from the dead, men will also have to admit the existence of a higher power – God.

In his discussion about the resurrection, McGarvey listed certain facts about the resurrection that are acknowledged by both friends and enemies of Christianity before he went on to sum up the crux of the matter:

> By the leading skeptics it is now admitted, first, that Jesus actually died and was buried; second, it is admitted that on or before the third morning his body disappeared from the tomb; third, that the disciples came to believe firmly that he arose from the dead. The exact issue has reference to these last two facts, and may be stated by the two questions, Did the body disappear by a resurrection, or in some other way? and Did the belief of the disciples originate from the fact of the resurrection, or from some other cause? [5]

Considering McGarvey's first question, we must ask: What happened to the body of Jesus? The options include the following:

(1) Jesus' body was stolen by His friends.

(2) Jesus' body was stolen by His enemies.

(3) Jesus' body was misplaced in a tomb other than the one considered to be His own.

(4) Jesus' body was not actually dead when placed within the tomb.

(5) Jesus' body was resurrected from the dead.

To presume that Jesus' body was stolen by His friends would be unacceptable on two counts. First, it fails to consider that the Jews made preparations to have the tomb guarded. Matthew 27:62-66 states:

> On the next day, which followed the Day of Preparation, the chief priests and Pharisees gathered together to Pilate, saying, "Sir, we remember, while He was still alive, how that deceiver said, 'After three days I will rise.' Therefore command that the tomb be made secure until the third day, lest His disciples come by night and steal Him away, and say to the people, 'He has risen from the dead.' So the last deception will be worse than the first."

> Pilate said to them, "You have a guard; go your way, make it as secure as you know how." So they went and made the tomb secure, sealing the stone and setting the guard.

Surely no one would argue that the ragged band of Jesus' followers could have successfully removed His body from a heavily guarded tomb.

Second, the criticism fails to consider the actions of the disciples after the supposed resurrection. Instead of living as if their leader was dead, the disciples claimed, in the face of great adversity, that Jesus was resurrected. In fact, they were willing to die rather than give up this belief. Thus, when warned by the Jewish leaders to keep quiet about Jesus of Nazareth, Peter and John responded, "Whether it is right in the sight of God to listen to you more than to God, you judge. For we cannot but speak the things which we have seen and heard" (Acts 4:19-20). That response, characteristic of Jesus' followers, is far from what one would expect from individuals merely propagating a lie.

Arguing that Jesus' enemies stole His body from the tomb also falls woefully short of providing us with a plausible alternative. Namely, there is no reason to believe that His enemies would have done so. First, it is ridiculous to conclude that those who would benefit most by Jesus' death would do something (such as remove His body from the tomb) that might lend credibility to His teachings. Second, it is ridiculous to conclude that His enemies, given the opportunity to stop the mouths of His followers, would have failed to do so. If they stole the body of Jesus, regardless of the reason, they would have presented it to quell the talk of the resurrection.

The third alternative, that Jesus' body was misplaced in a tomb other than that which was considered His own, is also fraught with problems. Primarily, it assumes, without reason, the ignorance of practically everyone involved in the burial – both friends and foes. Because Scripture teaches that Jesus' body was taken by Joseph of Arimathea and laid in "his new tomb" (Matthew 27:57-60), that the burial was witnessed by Mary Magdalene and the other Mary (v. 61), and that the tomb was sealed and guarded by His enemies, it is inconceivable to think that all the parties involved were mistaken about the location.

Finally, the alternative that states that Jesus was not actually dead when His body was placed within the tomb is perhaps the most ridiculous supposition of all. First, it stands in direct contradiction to the historical accounts of the event. Not only do all of the gospel accounts agree that Jesus died upon the cross, secular history corresponds to this fact as well. If nothing else, the testimony of John, who stood nearby the cross, should serve to verify Jesus' death:

> Then the soldiers came and broke the legs of the first and of the other who was crucified with Him. But when they came to Jesus and saw that He was already dead, they did not break His legs. But one of the soldiers pierced His side with a spear, and immediately blood and water came out. And he who has seen has testified, and his testimony is true; and he knows that he is telling the truth, so that you may believe (John 19:32-35).

With all of the possibilities regarding the question of the whereabouts of Jesus' body considered, the only solution that remains is to say that Jesus was resurrected. And this fact, of course, provides us with the only plausible answer to McGarvey's second question: "Did the belief of the disciples originate from the fact of the resurrection, or from some other cause?" What was it that motivated the disciples to preach about the risen Savior despite persecution? What was it that motivated Paul to change his life from persecuting Christians to being a persecuted Christian? It was the fact that Jesus arose from the dead. Describing this, Frank Morrison, in his classic book *Who Moved the Stone?*, wrote:

> Personally, I am convinced that no body of men or women could persistently and successfully have preached in Jerusalem a doctrine involving the vacancy of that tomb, without the grave itself being physically vacant. The facts were too recent; the tomb too close to that seething center of oriental life. Not all the make-believe in the world could have purchased the utter silence of antiquity or given to the records their impressive unanimity. Only the truth itself, in all its unavoidable simplicity, could have achieved that. [6]

Having shown that no reasonable possibility exists other than that Jesus arose from the grave and knowing that being resurrected from the dead defies both natural law and explanation, we have grounds to conclude that there must exist a supernatural power that orchestrated the resurrection – God.

## The Biblical Argument

It might seem strange to seek to prove the existence of God by appealing to the Bible. However, if it can be shown that the Bible has characteristics that could come only as a result of God, then God must exist. Thus, the biblical argument for God's existence holds that the Bible is a book beyond human production. Because this topic will be discussed in detail in later sections, it should suffice to say that the existence of fulfilled prophecies, scientific foreknowledge, historical accuracy, and unity despite having been written by more than 40 writers from various backgrounds over a period spanning some 1,600 years indicate that the Bible is the result of God.

Because of this, the Bible, which tells us about the qualities of God and provides us with details about the creation of the world, can be correctly used to point men to God. But sadly, men who desire to know about God often look for their answers in all the wrong places. With regard to this misdirection, Alexander Campbell's comments, taken from his debate with Robert Owen (1829), are worth noting:

Nothing astonishes me more than the impotency of philosophy in all matters and things pertaining to a spiritual system: to the origin and nature of all those relations in which mankind stand to the Creator and toward one another as immortal beings. And how men reared and educated within the precincts of revelation, can exhibit so many raw and undisciplined ideas of human nature, to say nothing of the future and unseen world, is still more astonishing. To hear all the skeptics, too, in one conclave assembled, declare their perfect ignorance of the fundamental springs and principles of all their own laws of nature; and, indeed, of the origin of all things and their destiny: to see them predicate all their system of infidelity of such acknowledged ignorance – and then upbraid Christianity, as if predicated of ignorance of God and man, is a contradiction, or inconsistency, for which I can find no parallel in the whole range of my acquaintance with men and things. If, as they confess, they neither know, nor can know, the origin of this earth and all things upon it, how or why do they presume to deny the Mosaic account of it!! They profess not to know anything about it; why, then, attempt to deny, or oppose the only account of it in the world, which without philosophy, but with the authority of the sacred historian, presents a credible history of it?[7]

When we consider the evidence that supports the resurrection of Jesus, and we couple that evidence with the knowledge that such an event could not have occurred unless God exists, we can conclude with certainty that there is a God. Although this line of reasoning is not how the argument from religious experience is traditionally presented, it is a variation that deserves consideration. At the same time, the existence of the Bible with the impressive characteristics that set it apart from the works of men, likewise points to the existence of God. But regardless of whether individuals admit that the resurrection occurred or that the Bible is a book that could not be produced by mere men, honest individuals must at least admit that if events such as the resurrection transpired and if the Bible is indeed a book that men could not produce, there must be a God. Because of this fact, these arguments cannot be ignored.

## Questions for Consideration

1. How is the argument from religious experience usually presented?

2. Why is this form of the argument subject to criticism?

3. How can the argument be structured to rescue it from this difficulty?

4. What event might be used to prove God's existence?

5. How does this approach compare to the other arguments used to prove God's existence?

6. Why would one use the Bible to prove God's existence?

7. How would you substantiate the argument that says the Bible is a book beyond human production?

## Chapter 5

# The Problem
# of Evil

Having presented the arguments commonly used to prove God's existence, we must now turn our attention to the objection presented most often by those who doubt there is a God – the problem of evil. Also known as the argument from evil, this line of reasoning attempts to prove that the God of the Bible cannot exist by pointing to the existence of evil and suffering in the world. As we consider this subject, we will take a closer look at evil, call attention to possible solutions to its existence, and consider how to deal with evil in light of Scripture.

## Introduction to the Problem

The problem of evil has existed in one form or another since the time of the philosopher Epicurus (341-270 B.C.). It was then proposed because he believed that "the evil with which human life is afflicted is irreconcilable with the idea of divine guidance in the universe." [1] In defining the problem, Epicurus wrote:

> God either wishes to take away evil, and is unable; or He is able, and is unwilling; or He is neither willing nor able, or He is both willing and able. If He is willing and is unable, He is feeble, which is not in accordance with the character of God; if He is able and unwilling, He is envious, which is equally at variance with God; if He is neither willing nor

able, He is both envious and feeble, and therefore not God; if He is both willing and able, which alone is suitable to God, from what source then are evils? Or why does He not remove them?[2]

John Hick aptly summarized the problem of evil: "If God is perfectly good, He must want to abolish all evil; if He is unlimitedly powerful, He must be able to abolish all evil: but evil exists; therefore either God is not perfectly good or He is not unlimitedly powerful."[3]

Regardless of whether you have ever faced the problem of evil in this form, it is likely that you might have been provoked to ask, as Francois Petit was, "How can God allow all this?" Or again, "If God existed, should we be seeing all this?"[4] Rather than examining the problem in its logical form, it is much more common for individuals to consider the sheer amount of suffering that seems to be present in the world and wonder whether a good, omnipotent God would allow such to exist. When viewed in this way, the problem of evil is transformed from a philosopher's argument into a practical question that deserves immediate attention.

The existence of suffering does not necessarily imply a logical inconsistency in the idea of God. Nevertheless, the problem of evil does stand as a plausible objection to God's existence that must be answered. This objection, presented as an argument, takes the following form:

1. There exist instances of intense suffering which an omnipotent, omniscient being could have prevented without thereby preventing the occurrence of any greater good.

2. An omniscient, wholly good being would prevent the occurrence of any intense suffering it could, unless it could not do so without thereby losing some greater good.

Therefore,

3. There does not exist an omnipotent, omniscient, wholly good being.[5]

## Solutions to the Problem

One prominent solution offered in response to the problem of evil was given by the German philosopher Gottfried Leibniz (1646-1716). Summarizing his position, Ed L. Miller described how Leibniz felt, saying that it would "be logically impossible to have a world without evil: Anything created by God would have to be less than God just by virtue of being dependent on him, and this means immediately that it must be less than perfect." [6] But just because the world must be less than perfect does not mean that Leibniz believed it to be less than the best of all possible worlds. In fact, he believed that God chose to create this world exactly as it is because it simply could not be improved:

> To overthrow this objection, therefore, it is sufficient to show
> that a world with evil might be better than a world without
> evil; but I have gone even farther in the work, and have even
> proved that this universe must be in reality better than every
> other possible universe. [7]

This, of course, does not mean that everything that happens in this world might be considered as the best possible event. It does, however, mean that given the entirety of the events of the world as a whole, God could not have created a better world. To understand Leibniz's solution, it must also be noted that he recognized a distinction between the kinds of evil in the world. Physical evil, or suffering, is part of the necessary structure of the world. Moral evil is quite different. It results from the conscious actions of individuals with free will. Leibniz correctly concluded that God cannot be blamed for moral evil that results from man's exercise of free will.

Although we could certainly take issue with at least some of Leibniz's approach, it is just as certain that much of his solution is quite valuable. In fact, when it is modified only slightly, it seems to become even more formidable. As John Hick wrote,

> The question whether this is the best possible world will
> then depend upon a prior question concerning God's pur-
> pose in creating man and setting him within the kind of world
> in which he finds himself. The best possible world will be
> that which serves the purpose that God is seeking to fulfill
> by means of it. [8]

Hick went on to identify God's purpose for the world as being a "vale of soul-making, designed as an environment in which finite persons may develop the more valuable qualities of moral personality." [9] In such a world, physical evils are necessary to help train the individuals who live therein and remind them of the brevity of life. Likewise, moral evils will also be present when men inevitably exercise their free will. Thus, if this solution is accepted, the existence of suffering and evil stop counting against God's existence and actually help to remind men of God's ultimate purpose – "bringing many sons to glory" (Hebrews 2:10).

In addition to the solution offered by Leibniz, there are many who argue that we must not discount the benefits of suffering. With this in mind, C.S. Lewis wrote, "God whispers to us in our pleasures, speaks in our conscience, but shouts in our pains: it is His megaphone to rouse a deaf world." [10] Accordingly, it is argued that those who are able to endure pain are stronger because of it. Adding credibility to this argument, the writer of Hebrews described the effect of suffering on Christ: "[T]hough He was a Son, yet He learned obedience by the things which He suffered. And having been perfected, He became the author of eternal salvation to all who obey Him" (Hebrews 5:8-9).

With that being said, the best way to answer the supposed problem of evil is to provide an adequate response to the following four questions.

(1) Is God omni-benevolent?

(2) Is God omnipotent?

(3) Does evil exist?

(4) Does the existence of evil necessarily imply that an omni-benevolent, omnipotent God cannot exist?

In answering the first two questions, we must turn to Scripture for our authority. The omni-benevolent nature of God is affirmed in 1 John 4:7-8: "Beloved, let us love one another, for love is of God; and everyone who loves is born of God and knows God. He who does not love does not know God, for God is love." Additionally, Paul described how God "desires all men to be saved and to come to the knowledge of the truth" (1 Timothy 2:4). This desire springs from the omni-benevolent nature of God.

Likewise, the omnipotent nature of God is affirmed in Scripture. The hosts of heaven declared, "Alleluia! For the Lord God Omnipotent reigns!" (Revelation 19:6). This, of course, does not mean that God is able to do that which cannot be done. But as C.S. Lewis correctly observed, "His Omnipotence means power to do all that is intrinsically possible, not to do the intrinsically impossible. You may attribute miracles to Him, but not nonsense."[11] In other words, whatever can be done is subject to God's power, and the failure to be able to do the impossible does not count against God's omnipotence.

In answering the third question, it must be granted that real evil does in fact exist in the form of sin. Thomas B. Warren set forth this view:

> I shall be concerned to uphold the view that sin (disobedience to God's will as revealed, we assume, in the Scriptures, that which contradicts sonship and brotherhood, that which involves the loss of fellowship with God) is the only real evil, that nothing subhuman is really evil, that man is responsible for his own sins, that evil (sin) really does exist, and that while it is the case that evil really does exist, it is not evil that there is evil.[12]

This, of course, does not mean that physical pain or suffering does not exist. It simply means that pain is not intrinsically evil.

> The mere fact that an action has resulted in pain is not sufficient ground to brand it as intrinsically evil. A physician is not evil (nor guilty of an evil action) when he inflicts pain in amputating a man's gangrenous foot. A mother is not evil (nor guilty of any evil action) when she spanks her small child for disobeying her in crossing a street which is heavily traveled. If pain per se were intrinsically evil, then every instance of pain (including those inflicted by kindly, skilled surgeons and by loving mothers) would be evil. Yet, such instances of inflicting pain are not evil. Why is this the case? It is the case because the motives and actions of those inflicting the pain were in harmony with the will of God. It seems clear, therefore, that no logical contradiction is involved in the infliction of pain by a perfectly good being. In fact, it seems that, in at least some circumstances, the inflicting of pain is the only thing which a good will can do.

Pain per se is neither intrinsically good nor intrinsically evil. "Evil" and "good" come into the picture only in relation to the will of the person who brought the action or state about, and in relation to the will of God – that is, only in relation to the contradiction of sonship and brotherhood, and thus, fellowship with God. [13]

Evil, then, is more than simply the "loss of good" [14] as some have supposed. It is the violation of God's law by beings with free will, and it exists beyond any doubt.

In answering the fourth question, we may conclude that the existence of evil (i.e., sin) does not imply that an omni-benevolent, omnipotent God cannot exist. On the contrary, it seems that the existence of real evil proves the existence of God implicitly. This is true because sin, by its very definition, is a transgression of God's law. Accordingly, 1 John 3:4 states, "Whoever commits sin also commits lawlessness, and sin is lawlessness." In other words, when man sins, he violates the law that exists by acting in a lawless fashion. The law that man violates must have its basis in God because it is impossible to have objective laws without an objective lawgiver. Thus, sin, the only intrinsic evil, actually proves God's existence rather than disproving it. As has already been stated, the difficulties that man must face are not evil themselves. Instead, they help man become stronger and serve to aid him in fulfilling the very purpose for which God created him – seeking after the Lord (see Acts 17:26-28).

## Scriptures to Consider

More important than any thoughts which man might present are the thoughts regarding suffering discussed in Scripture. Many passages and examples could be cited, but two should suffice. The first example is the account of Job found in the Old Testament. Those familiar with his life know that Job lost practically everything. In one day his vast wealth was taken from him, and his children died tragically. Eventually, his health also failed, his wife advised him to "Curse God and die!" (Job 2:9), and his friends accused him of wrongdoing. Despite these setbacks, Job maintained his belief in God and in the end benefited greatly because of his perseverance. James 5:11 states: "Indeed we count them blessed who endure. You have heard of the perseverance of Job and seen the end, intended by the Lord – that the Lord is very compassionate and merciful." Rather than charge God with wrong, James reveals that God used Job's trials to bring about good results. Regardless of whatever results might have been intended, Job developed the type of patience that is promised when we face trials in life (James 1:2-4).

A second example is found in the life of Paul. Describing his own physical suffering, Paul wrote:

> And lest I should be exalted above measure by the abundance of the revelations, a thorn in the flesh was given to me, a messenger of Satan to buffet me, lest I be exalted above measure. Concerning this thing I pleaded with the Lord three times that it might depart from me. And He said to me, "My grace is sufficient for you, for My strength is made perfect in weakness." Therefore most gladly I will rather boast in my infirmities, that the power of Christ may rest upon me. Therefore I take pleasure in infirmities, in reproaches, in needs, in persecutions, in distresses, for Christ's sake. For when I am weak, then I am strong (2 Corinthians 12:7-10).

Paul's suffering was so great that he was prompted to ask God to remove it on three different occasions. But each time God's answer was the same – "My grace is sufficient for you, for My strength is made perfect in weakness." In other words, God intended for Paul's weakness to help him grow stronger. Thus, rather than being an enemy to Paul, his thorn in the flesh was a friend in disguise. Paul's pain literally kept him humble and taught him more about the love of God. Noting this, Thomas B. Warren aptly wrote, "Because he had the 'thorn,' Paul reached and maintained spiritual heights which he would not have reached without it." [15]

Those who believe in the existence of God need not fear the problem of evil. If God created the world for a particular purpose, and if it can be shown that physical suffering helps to facilitate the purpose for which the world was created, then we may correctly conclude that the problem of evil does not count as evidence against the existence of God. To make this case, we should look no further than the words of the psalmist. He wrote: "It is good for me that I have been afflicted, that I may learn Your statutes" (Psalm 119:71). The problem of evil fails to consider that physical suffering can actually produce positive results. If nothing more, it often forces those who suffer to rely more upon God and less upon themselves.

## Questions for Consideration

1. What is the basis for the problem of evil?

2. How did Gottfried Leibniz approach the problem?

3. Do you agree or disagree with Leibniz's solution?

4. Do you believe that there are benefits to suffering? If so, what are they?

5. Reread Thomas B. Warren's description of evil on pages 41-42. How does Warren make the case that evil is more than just the absence of good?

6. What can we learn about suffering from the biblical accounts of Job and Paul?

7. Does God have a purpose for the creation? If so, what is that purpose?

8. Does suffering play a necessary role in helping man achieve the purpose that God desires for him?

## Chapter 6

# The Coherence of Theism

Those who wish to challenge Christianity commonly argue that God, as He is presented in the Bible, is self-contradictory. Charging that God cannot possess all of the attributes ascribed to Him in Scripture, critics conclude that Christian theism fails to be coherent and must therefore be rejected. But is this claim true? Can we show that the attributes, or essential properties, of God operate in conjunction with one another rather than in opposition? And most importantly, does Scripture really present an incoherent view of God? To answer these questions, we will examine the attributes of God as they are presented in Scripture, take a closer look at whether certain attributes of God are actually opposed to one another, and show that the description of God found within the Bible does not provide sufficient grounds for rejecting His existence.

## The Attributes of God

When we claim to believe in the God revealed in the Bible, we are claiming "to believe in the existence of a supremely good being, creator of but independent of the world, omnipotent, omniscient, eternal … and self-existent." [1] And although it would certainly be possible to add other attributes to this list, such as omnipresence, the ones mentioned are indisputably affirmed in Scripture. For that reason, we must notice what the Bible says about each of these attributes or characteristics before considering some of the objections raised against them.

It is obvious to anyone who has ever read the Bible that God is described as being supremely good. Whether it was Abraham asking: "Shall not the Judge of all the earth do right?" (Genesis 18:25), or the prophet Habakkuk noting, "You are of purer eyes than to behold evil, and cannot look on wickedness" (Habakkuk 1:13), those acquainted with Jehovah God recognized His infinite goodness. Passages throughout the New Testament only add to the idea that God is supremely good. It was, according to John 3:16, the love of God that motivated Him to send His Son to die for humanity. John even went so far as to say that God is love. He wrote, "Beloved, let us love one another, for love is of God; and everyone who loves is born of God and knows God. He who does not love does not know God, for God is love" (1 John 4:7-8). Truly, the supremely good nature of God is seen, not only in His desire for all men to be saved (1 Timothy 2:4), but in His willingness to provide every good gift to those who walk uprightly (Psalm 84:11).

Just as Scripture describes God as a supremely good being, it also describes Him as the creator of our world. Appropriately, the Bible begins: "In the beginning God created the heavens and the earth" (Genesis 1:1). It is significant to note that Scripture makes a clear distinction between the Creator and the creation. For example, Hebrews 11:3 states: "By faith we understand that the worlds were framed by the word of God, so that the things which are seen were not made of things which are visible." Because God is described as the builder and the world as the thing He built (Hebrews 3:4) and because the creation is said to declare God's handiwork (Psalm 19:1), it is clear that God created the world and exists independently from it.

Another attribute of God asserted in Scripture is that of omnipotence. Describing Himself to Abraham, God said, "I am Almighty God; walk before Me and be blameless" (Genesis 17:1). The prophet Jeremiah stated, "Ah, Lord God! Behold, You have made the heavens and the earth by Your great power and outstretched arm. There is nothing too hard for You" (Jeremiah 32:17). And Paul, describing God's creation, noted that His "eternal power" could be known by all (Romans 1:20).

The omniscience of God is also asserted in Scripture. By just reading from Isaiah, we find that man cannot teach God anything (Isaiah 40:13), His "understanding is unsearchable" (v. 28), He declares the new things "[b]efore they spring forth" (42:9), and He is able to declare the end of a thing from its beginning (46:10). When we add to these passages the many prophecies found in the Old and New Testaments, it is clear that God's knowledge is not limited by the boundaries of time. Just as God's power enables Him to do all that can be done, He likewise knows all that can be known.

Adding to the list of God's attributes, Scripture affirms that He is eternal and by virtue of this infinite nature, self-existent. This means that God's existence does not depend on anything else. God is not a contingent being. John implied this when he wrote: "In the beginning was the Word, and the Word was with God, and the Word was God" (John 1:1). And Paul, in offering praise to God, wrote, "Now to the King eternal, immortal, invisible, to God who alone is wise, be honor and glory forever and ever. Amen" (1 Timothy 1:17). As we consider whether the biblical concept of God makes sense, despite whatever else might be said, we must conclude that the Bible affirms the existence of an eternal creator who is supremely good, all-powerful and all-knowing.

## Do the Attributes of God Oppose One Another?

As has already been noted, the problem of evil, which actually attempts to place the attributes of supreme goodness and omnipotence in opposition to one another, is the main argument used by both atheists and agnostics in their attempt to disprove the existence of God. But if the problem of evil can be answered in a rational manner, those who disbelieve have only one other course that they can pursue – they can attempt to show that the very concept of God is self-contradictory or incoherent.

One common approach is to question how God can be all-knowing and, at the same time, allow man the freedom to act as he chooses. Formulating this into an argument, William L. Rowe wrote:

> 1. God knows before we are born everything we will do.
> 2. If God knows before we are born everything we will do, then it is never in our power to do otherwise.
> 3. If it is never in our power to do otherwise, then there is no human freedom.
> Therefore,
> 4. There is no human freedom. [2]

Although Rowe's conclusion is accepted by those who adhere to the doctrine of John Calvin, it is equally unacceptable to many atheists and theists. Thus, because men generally recognize the existence of human freedom, some feel that this dilemma shows that God simply cannot be omniscient in the way that the Bible describes Him. And if it is true that God is not omniscient, the concept of God presented in Scripture begins to unravel.

In hopes of answering this supposed dilemma, some have tried to argue that God has the ability to choose to limit His knowledge. According to this approach, God restrains or limits Himself from knowing certain things that will occur in the future. Ronald Nash describes this view:

> This scenario suggests that God possesses only partial knowledge about the future because He freely chooses to restrict His knowledge of the future in order to preserve some measure of human freedom. This picture would be compatible with a somewhat different theory according to which God has unerring knowledge of some specific future events, namely, those which He has decreed must happen. But of future events that are not the subject of divine decree, God's knowledge is impossible. [3]

Noted Bible commentator Adam Clarke had a similar approach:

> As God's omnipotence implies the power to do all things, so God's omniscience implies his power to know all things; but we must take heed that we meddle not with the infinite free-agency of the Eternal Being. Though God can do all things, he does not [do] all things ... God is omniscient, and can know all things, but does it follow from this that he must know all things? Is he not as free in the volitions of his wisdom as he is in the volitions of his power? [4]

In response to this approach, there seem to be at least two problems that need clarification. First, why does God foreknow some things (such as those things that He has prophesied) and not foreknow other things? And if God has the ability to limit what He knows about future contingencies, how does He determine what to know and what to refrain from knowing? More specifically, must God know a particular thing and then forget it in order for the approach to be accurate? If so, there seems to be a great difficulty with this approach.

Second, it seems that the argument that equates omnipotence and omniscience assumes too much. It is true that God does not do all of the things within His power, but this does not count against His omnipotence. It does not necessarily follow that God can choose to limit His knowledge and still remain omniscient. It seems that omniscience differs from omnipotence in one very important way: to be omniscient, one must know all things and not simply have the potential to do so. Thus, if an omniscient being limited His knowledge of even one thing, He would cease to be all-knowing. Omnipotence, however, only requires that one have the power to do all that can be done, not that one has already done everything within the realm of possibility.

Dismissing that approach, we must now propose another alternative. It is certainly possible for God to have unlimited foreknowledge of man's actions and man retain his freedom if it can be shown that God exists outside the realm of time (see 2 Peter 3:8). When viewed in this way, the problem ceases to exist because God can survey events – whether past, present or future – from His timeless perspective without forcing the events to occur. Recognizing this, William Rowe noted, "For although God's foreordaining something makes that something happen, his foreknowing does not make it happen. Things occur not because God knows them; rather, he foreknows them because they occur." [5] He then added: God's knowledge of what is past and future is just like the knowledge that we may have of something that is happening in the present. Being above time, God takes in all time with one glance just as we who are in time may with a glance take in something that is happening in the present. [6]

Thus, we may rationally conclude that no contradiction exists between God's omniscience and man's freedom. "The distinction between knowledge and foreknowledge is only in us. There is no such difference in God." [7]

Another attempt made by those skeptical of God's existence is to argue that the supremely good nature of God and the existence of eternal hell are incompatible. In essence, they charge that God cannot be supremely good and allow hell to exist. But is this a fair assumption? For several reasons, it seems not. First, it is incorrect to ignore certain teachings of Scripture and recognize others. One cannot ascribe love to God and fail to recognize His wrath (see John 3:36; Romans 11:22). Second, we cannot make God's attributes compete with one another, for His attributes jointly control His actions. B.B. Warfield correctly stated, "God is not part God, a God here and there, with some but not all the attributes which belong to true God: he is God altogether, God through and through, all that God is and all that God ought to be." [8] Third, it fails to consider that God's goodness (which is partly comprised by His justice) requires Him to punish those who reject His will. Like the parent who, because of love, punishes his or her children when they disobey, God punishes mankind because of His love and not despite it.

So how then can a supremely good God allow souls to be eternally punished in hell? He can do so because of the terrible nature of sin. According to Scripture, sin separates man from God (Isaiah 59:1-2), and the wages of sin is death (Romans 6:23). Recognizing how terrible sin is, Charles Hodge asserted that "we are incompetent judges of the penalty which sin deserves. We have no adequate apprehension of its inherent guilt, of the dignity of the person against whom it is committed, or of the extent of the evil which it is suited to produce." [9] Thus, rather than counting the existence of hell against God, we can rationally count it as a credit toward His goodness.

## A God of Harmony

In view of the foregoing discussion, we may rationally conclude that the description of God found within the Bible does, in fact, make sense. Having shown that we cannot isolate the attributes of God and place them in competition with one another, we may rightly conclude that God's essence depends upon all of His attributes cooperating jointly. Rather than existing in an antagonistic manner, the attributes of God cooperate in a harmonious fashion to make Him what He is.

## Questions for Consideration
1. What is meant by the charge that the God presented in the Bible is self-contradictory?

2. What is an attribute?

3. Why is it important to affirm that God possesses the attributes ascribed to Him in Scripture?

4. What does the term "omniscient" mean?

5. How is it possible for God to possess knowledge in the fullest sense of the term and man still be free to act as He chooses?

6. Does the existence of hell count against the goodness of God?

7. How could one use the existence of hell to argue in favor of God's goodness?

8. Describe how the attributes of God must be studied.

## Chapter 7

# The Bible's Claims of Inspiration

Regardless of how one might view religion in general, that view is shaped by what one thinks about the Bible. If the Bible is considered to be nothing more than a collection of ancient documents written by men, it will have little, if any, influence upon those who read it. If, however, it is considered to be the inspired Word of God, those who spend time studying it will seek to alter their lives according to its mandates. That, of course, is not to say that everyone who considers the Bible to be God's Word always obeys it. But at the least, those who view the Bible to be from God feel that when they disobey its precepts, they have done something that is objectively wrong.

In the next two chapters, we will take a closer look at how men ought to view the Bible. Is the Bible the Word of God? Or is it merely a collection of legends and fables? Is the Bible accurate in its many assertions? Or is it filled with egregious errors? These, and other important questions, will be answered. Additionally, we will examine some of the many claims that are made within Scripture, define what is meant by inspiration, and look at the proofs commonly used to show that the Bible must be the product of God.

## Claims the Bible Makes

It is obvious that just because someone might claim something, that claim is not necessarily true. In fact, claims, in order to be taken seriously, must be substantiated. With that in mind, it might seem strange to begin a study of whether the Bible is inspired by looking at the various claims found within its pages. Nevertheless, if it can be shown that the Bible claims to be inspired and that it declares itself the book to which men must turn for guidance, it gives the study a certain sense of importance. So what does the Bible claim for itself?

**(1) The Bible claims to be inspired of God.** Paul wrote, "All Scripture is given by inspiration of God, and is profitable for doctrine, for reproof, for correction, for instruction in righteousness, that the man of God may be complete, thoroughly equipped for every good work" (2 Timothy 3:16-17). It is significant that the term "Scripture," used by Paul in this passage, can reference both the Old and New Testaments. [1] And it is also important to note that phrases such as "Thus says the Lord," "The Lord has spoken," "The word of the Lord," and "The Lord spoke" are found hundreds of times throughout the Bible.

**(2) The Bible claims to have been written by individuals who were directed by the Holy Spirit.** Peter made this clear when he wrote, "knowing this first, that no prophecy of Scripture is of any private interpretation, for prophecy never came by the will of man, but holy men of God spoke as they were moved by the Holy Spirit" (2 Peter 1:20-21). In essence, Peter argued that Scripture does not contain the mere ideas of men. Instead, Scripture was recorded by individuals who were moved by the influence of the Holy Spirit. This truth is reinforced when one considers what Paul wrote in his letter to the Ephesians:

> For this reason I, Paul, the prisoner of Christ Jesus for you Gentiles – if indeed you have heard of the dispensation of the grace of God which was given to me for you, how that by revelation He made known to me the mystery (as I have briefly written already, by which, when you read, you may understand my knowledge in the mystery of Christ), which in other ages was not made known to the sons of men, as it has now been revealed by the Spirit to His holy apostles and prophets (Ephesians 3:1-5).

**(3) The Bible claims to contain all the information that we need to live faithful lives.** Whether it was Paul asserting that Scripture is able to make us "complete, thoroughly equipped for every good work"

(2 Timothy 3:17), or Peter arguing that Scripture contains "all things that pertain to life and godliness" (2 Peter 1:3), it is clear that the Bible claims to contain all the information that man needs to be faithful to God. This claim, of course, is significant for a number of reasons. In particular, if it is true, then other sources which claim to provide additional revelation from God cannot be taken seriously. Both the book of Mormon and the Koran fall in this category. Additionally, if the claim is warranted, men have no right to make either additions to or subtraction from Scripture (see Deuteronomy 4:2; Proverbs 30:6; Revelation 22:18-19).

**(4) The Bible claims to be the final revelation from God.** This claim logically follows from the preceding claim. If it is true that the Bible contains all the information needed for man to live a life pleasing to God, it must be true that God will not provide any additional information to man. That, of course, is why Jesus charged that His commands should be taught "even to the end of the age" (Matthew 28:20) and that His words will be used to judge men in the last day (John 12:48). It is also why Jude admonished his readers "to contend earnestly for the faith which was once for all delivered to the saints" (Jude 3). In view of this, it is no wonder that Paul argued that neither men nor angels have a right to "preach any other gospel" (Galatians 1:8-9).

**(5) The Bible claims to be powerful.** The writer of Hebrews said, "For the word of God is living and powerful, and sharper than any two-edged sword, piercing even to the division of soul and spirit, and of joints and marrow, and is a discerner of the thoughts and intents of the heart" (4:12). The Bible's power is certainly seen in Jesus' claim that His words will never be destroyed (Matthew 24:35), but it is seen most clearly in its claim to be able to save man from his sins. Accordingly, James wrote, "Therefore lay aside all filthiness and overflow of wickedness, and receive with meekness the implanted word, which is able to save your souls. But be doers of the word, and not hearers only, deceiving yourselves" (James 1:21-22).

**(6) The Bible claims to be the standard to which men must turn to determine what is right or wrong.** The Bereans of the first century were complimented for doing this very thing. Luke described how they "were more fair-minded than those in Thessalonica, in that they received the word with all readiness, and searched the Scriptures daily to find out whether these things were so" (Acts 17:11).

No doubt other claims found within the Word of God could be added to the foregoing list. Nevertheless, these should adequately motivate us to consider carefully whether the Bible is inspired. If it is, its claims must be taken seriously; if it is not, it is filled with lies.

## The Meaning of Inspiration

Before offering proof for the inspiration of the Bible, we must clarify what is meant by "inspiration." Found only in 2 Timothy 3:16, the phrase "inspiration of God" comes from the Greek word, θεόπνευστος. That word itself comes "from θεὸς God and πνεῖν to breathe. [Thus, it means] God-Breathed." [2] Wayne Jackson simply noted, "It is an affirmation that God is the ultimate author of the Bible."

Nevertheless, Jackson realized that "inspiration" is a difficult concept for man to grasp:

> Inspiration cannot be explained precisely in a manner that human understanding can fathom completely. In some fashion, God was able to use certain men, preserving their personal literary abilities and traits, yet overseeing the process so that the exact will of the divine mind was conveyed through the human instrument (1 Corinthians 2:11ff). [3]

Describing the inspiration process, Keith Mosher wrote:

> The Bible writers were "inspired" not just in some intuitive way, but in a way that ensured that what they penned would **be** God's message. The message was "God-breathed." The Holy Spirit "moved" those ancients to write, and the writers submitted their minds and wills to the Spirit (2 Peter 1:20-21). The writer's normal cognitive functions, however, were not abandoned as if they were mere dictation machines, for their styles and thought processes were maintained as they wrote. This is "verbal" inspiration but not "dictation." God can and did use words that the writer would already know, but the writer would not pen his own message but God's.

> The product of the inspiration process is **revelation** that is completely free from error (inerrancy). Inspiration (God's act) uncovered (revealed) truth for man … .

God inspired, and man wrote. The result of this process is the **verbal** (words), **plenary** (every word), **inerrant** (errorless writings), **authoritative** (the words **are** from God) Bible. [Emphasis in original] [4]

Regardless of whatever else might be said about inspiration, the view that we take with regard to Scripture ought to mirror the way that our Savior viewed it. Pointing to the way Jesus responded to Satan when He was tempted, Wayne Jackson wrote:

> When the suggestion was made that he convert stones into bread to stay his hunger, the Saviour replied: "It is written, Man shall not live by bread alone, but by every word that proceedeth out of the mouth of God." (Matthew 4:4.) He was quoting Deuteronomy 8:3. Twice more he stopped the Devil's mouth with "It is written ..." citing Deuteronomy 6:13, 16. In declaring, "It is written," Jesus employed the Greek *perfect tense*, denoting completed action with abiding results. He thus declares that God's words were written and remain so! [Emphasis in original] [5]

Rather than portraying Scripture in a manner that allowed it to be subject to various interpretations, Jesus perceived that it settled the matters it addressed. That, of course, can be true only if it is from God and not man. Thus, inspiration refers to the process in which the Holy Spirit revealed God's message to individuals who faithfully recorded it. Those faithful recordings are the Words of God.

## Proofs for Inspiration

With the claims of the Bible set forth and with the term "inspiration" defined, we can make the case for inspiration. Why should we believe that the Bible is the product of God? To answer this question, a number of proofs will be considered. Included within this number are fulfilled prophecies, accuracy, unity, the quality of writing and relevance.

Fulfilled prophecies prove the inspiration of the Bible. George Dehoff claims, "No stronger proof not only of the truthfulness but of the inspiration of the writers of the Bible can be found than prophecy and its fulfillment." [6] But what counts as true prophecy? At first glance, one might answer that question by saying that prophecy is predicting the future. Such an answer, however, falls short of getting at the true nature of biblical prophecy. Noting this, Alexander Campbell made the following argument in his debate with Robert Owen:

> The foretelling of future events depends upon a knowledge of them; or of the causes and connections of things which, from established principles, necessarily issue in certain results. All men are possessed of a certain species of this sort of knowledge. They have a data which enables them not only to conjecture, but even to foreknow with certainty what shall come to pass. This data is either the result of experience, of reasoning upon well-established principles, or upon testimony. We know that all the living shall die; that the trees will bud and blossom in spring; that the moon will change; a comet appear; or that an clipse [sic] of the sun will happen on a certain day. Men of extraordinary sagacity can penetrate into futurity, and sometimes guess, conjecture, and even foretell, upon a large accumulation of probabilities, certain political events. But still the limitations and utmost bounds of this knowledge are very narrow; and comparatively few are the events future of which men can speak with certainty. [7]

There is more to genuine prophecy than just gathering facts and offering an educated guess. Batsell Barrett Baxter wrote, "Prophecy deals with events and human affairs which do not happen in a causal order, but are unpredictable. A prophecy must be more than just a good guess. It must possess sufficient accuracy as to be capable of verification." [8] Dehoff added:

> The event must be beyond the power of man to foresee; it must not be a vision of hope nor a result of fear; it must not be a scientific or political forecast. The prediction must be written before the event occurs and must be applicable to it. The language of the prophecy must be clear and the fulfillment plain. [9]

That being said, three facts about prophecy must be considered. First, the Bible contains hundreds of prophecies about a variety of subjects: specific people, natural disasters, nations and many other events spanning both the Old and New Testaments. Second, these prophecies are very specific in nature. Rather than being so vague that one could count just about anything as a fulfillment to a prophecy, the prophecies found in the Bible contain specific details. Whether it was Micah foretelling the place of the Savior's birth – Bethlehem (Micah 5:2), Daniel identifying the nations that would rise in succession to one another (Daniel 2:36-45), or Zechariah specifying the details of the Savior's betrayal (Zechariah 11:12-13), the prophecies found within the Bible are certainly clear. Third, the Bible argues that even one false prophecy will cause credibility to be lost. According to Deuteronomy 18:22, "[W]hen a prophet speaks in the name of the Lord, if the thing does not happen or come to pass, that is the thing which the Lord has not spoken; the prophet has spoken it presumptuously; you shall not be afraid of him." Coming from a source containing well over 1,000 prophecies, such a high standard for credibility seems to express the ultimate confidence.

In view of these facts, it seems reasonable to argue that if the Bible not only predicts but specifically foretells events years before their fulfillment, that action constitutes proof of divine inspiration. Notice these examples of prophecies and their fulfillment:

## BIBLE PROPHECIES AND THEIR FULFILLMENT

| Prophecy | Fulfillment |
|---|---|
| 1. Christ was to be born of a virgin (Isaiah 7:14). | Matthew 1:22-23 |
| 2. Christ was to be born in Bethlehem (Micah 5:2). | Matthew 2:5-6 |
| 3. Christ was to be a prophet like Moses (Deuteronomy 18:14-18). | Acts 3:20-23 |
| 4. Christ was to be sold for 30 pieces of silver (Zechariah 11:12). | Matthew 26:15 |
| 5. Christ was to be crucified (Psalm 22:16-18; Isaiah 53:1-12). | John 19:16-37 |

6. Christ was to be resurrected
   (Psalm 16:10).                                    Acts 2:25-31

7. Christ was to ascend into the heavens
   (Psalm 68:18).                                    Mark 16:19

8. The world would be blessed through
   Abraham's seed (Genesis 12:3).                    Matthew 1:1-16

9. The church would begin in Jerusalem
   (Isaiah 2:2-4).                                   Acts 2

10. The church would begin during the
    Roman Empire (Daniel 2:44).                      Acts 25:9-12

The Bible is filled with claims about its inspiration and importance. We have clarified what is meant by the term "inspiration," and this chapter discussed one of the major proofs offered in support the Bible's claims – fulfilled prophecy. It is obviously beyond the ability of men to make precise predictions about individuals, places and events several hundred years beforehand, so the existence of genuine prophecy in the Scripture helps to substantiate the claims that the Bible makes regarding its origin. In the next chapter, we will continue the case for inspiration by considering the Bible's accuracy, unity, quality of writing and relevance.

## Questions for Consideration

1. How does the way we view the Bible affect the way we view religion in general?

2. Why are the claims found in the Bible relevant to a study of whether the Bible is inspired?

3. What does the term "inspiration" mean?

4. Describe your understanding of how "inspiration" works.

5. How did Jesus view the Scriptures?

6. Why is prophecy more than just predicting the future?

7. Cite some specific prophecies found within the Bible.

8. Why is fulfilled prophecy considered to be a proof of inspiration?

## Chapter 8

# Proving the Bible's Inspiration

It is certainly possible for an individual to produce a well-written, accurate, consistent and relevant book. Because of this, it might seem strange to find these characteristics being used to prove the Bible's inspiration. After all, if man can write a book on his own that is consistent and accurate, why should one believe that these characteristics identify a book that could come only from God?

To answer, we must consider that the Bible's accuracy is not merely based upon details about which we are currently aware. It also contains accurate details about many things that were certainly unknown to its authors. The same thing, of course, could be said about the quality of writing, unity and relevance of the Bible. If the Bible was poorly written, if it contained contradictions, or if it were not designed to meet the needs of man, individuals would dispute its claims.

## Proofs for Inspiration

**Accuracy proves the inspiration of the Bible.** Although it is not the purpose of the Bible to serve as a textbook in any particular academic field, it is nonetheless true that statements found within the Bible do introduce a variety of academic facts. Importantly, many of these facts were set forth long before they were discovered by men. So whether the Bible is addressing a historical matter, a scientific fact, or a geographical area, the statements contained within it are found to be accurate.

The significance of this truth must not escape our attention. In fact, it is utterly unthinkable that a group of writers, especially if many were relatively uneducated, would be able to produce a work that proves to be accurate in every area that it addresses. Yet this is the very thing that the Bible writers did! Not only have the explicit prophecies that they recorded proved to be true, but incidental statements that they wrote have also withstood the intense scrutiny of critics. One might presumably argue that a man could, given limited subject matter with which he was well acquainted, produce a work free from error. But to argue that the writers of the Bible, who addressed a vast number of topics, were able, without any outside help, to produce a work of the magnitude and quality of the Bible goes beyond even the loftiest expectations. Therefore, the only explanation for such accuracy is to say that the authors of the Bible were inspired by God.

In order to add weight to our claim that accuracy proves the Bible's inspiration, we would do well to consider several areas in which this accuracy is found. One such area is the field of science. Although it is certainly the case that modern science has discovered a great number of truths through its various methods, it is just as certain that many of these facts were revealed in Scripture hundreds, if not thousands, of years before their scientific discovery. As Wayne Jackson said, "One of the most arresting evidences of the inspiration of the Bible is the great number of scientific truths that have lain hidden within its pages for thirty centuries or more, only to be discovered by man's enterprise within the last few centuries or even years." [1] This phenomenon is often called scientific foreknowledge. Providing one example, George W. Dehoff wrote:

> Herbert Spencer (1820-1903) first announced that there are only five "manifestations of the unknowable" in existence – time, force, action, space and matter – and that all else is based on these fundamentals ... Moses wrote: "In the beginning," time; "God," force; "created," action; "the heavens," space; "and the earth," matter. Thus Moses put all five scientific fundamentals in the first verse of Genesis and they are in the same order as announced by Herbert Spencer. How could Moses do this? The answer must be that God told Moses what to write. [2]

Other common examples include the Bible's description of the earth as being spherical (Isaiah 40:22), its description of the earth hanging on nothing (Job 26:7), its allusion to the paths that run through the sea (Psalm 8:8), and its description of the importance of blood (Leviticus 17:11). What is perhaps just as impressive about the Bible's accuracy regarding scientific facts is its omission of ideas commonly promoted in ancient times.

> [W]e do not find the superstitions and wrong notions concerning scientific matters which were current in ancient times incorporated into the Scriptures. How easy it would have been for Moses to have slipped at one point or another, by including such things as the then believed hypotheses that the earth was flat and rested upon the back of some great turtle or some great elephant. The most natural thing would have been for the various writers to have included many superstitions which later would have been proved false. The absence of these is impressive evidence that God must have guided and superintended the writers. [3]

The following chart, developed from Wayne Jackson's book, *Fortify Your Faith*, introduces many of the scientific principles revealed within Scripture. [4]

## SCIENTIFIC FOREKNOWLEDGE AND THE BIBLE

*The Bible and Astronomy*
• The earth is spherical in shape (Proverbs 8:27; Isaiah 40:22).
• The earth is suspended in space (Job 26:7).
• Stars are innumerable (Jeremiah 33:22).

*The Bible and Geology*
• The earth evidences a sedimentary origin (Genesis 1:2).

*The Bible and Oceanography*
• The seas were created with a common bed (Genesis 1:9).
• There are streams or paths in the seas (Psalm 8:8).
• The ocean floors are coursed by canyons (Job 38:16; 2 Samuel 22:16).

*The Bible and Meteorology*
• The water cycle involving evaporation, transportation, condensation and gravitation is suggested (Job 36:27-28; Ecclesiastes 1:7).

*The Bible and Physics*
• Neither matter nor energy is presently being created (Genesis 2:1).
• The universe is running down or wearing out (Isaiah 51:6).
• Light requires time to travel through space and thus exists in a path (Job 38:24).

*The Bible and Biology*
• Life does not arise spontaneously (Acts 17:25).
• Living things reproduce according to the laws of heredity (Genesis 1:11-12, 21, 24).

*The Bible and Medicine*
• Sanitation laws imply germs (Deuteronomy 23:12-14).
• Life is in the blood (Leviticus 17:11).
• All nations share a common physical unity (Acts 17:26).
• The eighth day is ideal for circumcision (Genesis 17:12).

A second area in which the Bible has proven to be completely accurate is the field of history. To understand why historical accuracy counts as a proof for the inspiration of the Bible, one must realize that it is truly unusual for a book covering any appreciable time period to provide historical records and data in an error-free manner. The genealogical records that exist throughout this country testify to this fact. Yet the historical records found within the Bible, including long genealogical lists, have withstood the onslaught of antagonists time after time.

Those skeptical of the accounts of history found within the Bible question the existence of particular individuals or places. For example:

> [S]keptical scholars denied the existence of such a place as the land of Goshen, where the Bible tells us Israel dwelt, and they scoffed at the idea of Israel's oppression in making brick with straw. Not only has the name Goshen been found in the inscriptions, but the ruins of granaries in Pythom and Raamses reveal the fact that in the lower courses the bricks were made with straw, while in the upper portions

they were made without straw. A recent discovery confirms Ex. 1:11 in an inscription of Ramses II, which says he built the city of Raamses with Semitic labor. [5]

Another well-known example deals with the existence of the Hittite nation. Because there was no mention of this nation in sources outside the Bible, particularly in Greek and Roman histories, critics in the 19th century used the Bible's affirmation of the Hittite nation against it. Nevertheless, those critics were silenced when the Hittite city of Hattusas was unearthed in Turkey in the early part of the 20th century. Bill Humble says, "Since the discoveries at Hattusas, articles relating to the Hittites have been found in other lands." [6] These discoveries prompted this entry in the *International Standard Bible Encyclopedia*:

> Thus emerged from the shades of obscurity one of the greatest nations of the ancient world. Twenty-five years ago some of the foremost orientalists did not believe in the existence of a Hittite nation. Today it is seen that Hatti formed a worthy third with two other great nations, Egypt and Babylonia-Assyria. [7]

It is important to note that rather than showing the Bible to be inaccurate, archaeology has only served to confirm the historical accounts found within the Bible. With this in mind, Humble wrote:

> But thanks to the many discoveries of archaeology, Moses and Abraham, Noah and Joseph, the Hittites and other ancient people also live again. The Bible is not a book of myth and legend; it is a trustworthy record of real people, real cities, real events. The discoveries of archaeology have given us many proofs – "external evidences" that the Bible is historically accurate, trustworthy, when it records the deeds of these real people in a real past. [8]

A third area in which the Bible has shown itself to be reliable is in its reporting of geographical locations. For example, Luke described how Paul and Barnabas fled from Iconium "to Lystra and Derbe, cities of Lycaonia" (Acts 14:6). Because ancient geography held that Iconium was a city of Lycaonia, "[t]his passage was considered by some Bible critics to be a typical example of the lack of local exactitude by the author of Acts, and thus evidence against divine inspiration." [9] Luke's account, however, was eventually shown to be accurate by the archaeologist Sir William Ramsay. He demonstrated that "Iconium was not part of Lycaonia. Rather, it belonged to Phrygia, an entirely different district of Asia Minor." [10] As in other instances, the biblical account was found to be accurate.

**Unity proves the inspiration of the Bible.** When we consider the Bible in its completed form, it is utterly amazing that a group of 40 individuals from various backgrounds, separated both by time (some 1,600 years) and location, were able to produce a book that is harmonious and free from contradiction. Whether it is the Old Testament pointing to the coming Messiah, the gospels describing the life of Christ, or the remainder of the New Testament looking forward to His return, it is obvious that the Bible is unified in describing the Savior of mankind. This unity can also be seen in the various themes of the Bible. Keith Mosher Sr. argued that unity existed in seven areas in the Bible: structure, doctrine, prophecy, ethics, its organic sense – meaning that all the books are necessary to form the whole of the Bible and that they all provide a single life principle, soberness and expression. [11] He then surmised:

> It is more reasonable to conclude Divine inspiration for the Bible based on the above studies on its unified nature than that the Book is the product of many minds writing without God's guidance over long centuries. One must account for unity of structure, doctrine, prophecy, ethics, life-principle, soberness, and expression in some way. Trying to solve this issue of biblical unity without inspiration will prove to be an impossible task. [12]

Surely unity stands as a proof for the inspiration of God!

**The quality of writing proves the inspiration of the Bible.** Certainly the Bible is a unique book. One of the reasons for its uniqueness is the style in which it is written. This style has been used to give weight to the idea that the Bible is inspired by God. Consider these points raised by J.W. McGarvey in his book *Evidences of Christianity*:

(1) *Dramatic form of narration.* McGarvey noted: "[The New Testament writers] allow all of the actors in the scenes in which they describe to

play their several parts without a word of comment, without an expression of approval or disapproval, and entirely without those attempts at analysis of character in which other historians indulge."

(2) *Impartiality regarding the facts.* Although we might tend to leave out our failures or shortcomings if we were writing a historical account, this was not true of the biblical records. McGarvey described how the biblical authors spoke "with as little reserve concerning the sins and follies of themselves and their friends as of the wicked deeds of their enemies." [13] Not only did they record the treachery of Judas, but they recorded the failures of Peter as well.

(3) *Brevity.* Although men today write entire volumes recounting singular events, the Bible covers the history of the world from its creation until after the death of Christ and can be held easily in one hand! It is almost unthinkable that someone today would write a biography and fail to chronicle the first few years of the subject's life. Yet this is the very thing the biographers of Christ did. It is also difficult to read a biographical account and not find a description of the subject's physical appearance within that work, but not one of the four gospel writers describes the appearance of Jesus. When we consider why certain events were not recorded in the Bible or why certain events found there are not given in more detail, we are reminded of how John closed his gospel account: "And there are also many other things that Jesus did, which if they were written one by one, I suppose that even the world itself could not contain the books that would be written. Amen" (John 21:25).

(4) *The assumption of infallibility.* No matter how difficult the theme under consideration, the authors of the Bible never left the impression that their conclusions might be wrong. Instead, "on all subjects and on all occasions they speak with unhesitating confidence, never admitting the possibility of a mistake." [14]

**The relevance of the Bible proves its inspiration.** Regardless of whether man is facing a mental, physical, spiritual or social problem, the Bible is the book to which he may turn to find help. This, of course, is what one would expect from a book that claims to be from God.

Addressing mental issues, the Bible teaches man to maintain the proper perspective (Matthew 6:33; Ecclesiastes 12:13-14). It likewise describes how one can handle emotional distress by providing instructions to help avoid worry (Matthew 6:25-34) and by setting forth the proper views of pain, suffering and death (Job; Romans 8:18). Regarding our physical health, the Bible teaches us that our bodies belong to God (1 Corinthians 6:19-20), and that we must avoid certain things that harm our bodies (Proverbs 23:29-33; 1 Corinthians 6:18).

Addressing spiritual issues, the Bible teaches us that God loves us and sent Jesus to die in our place (John 3:16). In addition, it teaches us what we must do to be saved (Romans 10:17; Hebrews 11:6; Acts 8:37-38; 2:38; 22:16), that we can overcome temptations (1 Corinthians 10:13), and that eternity awaits us all (Matthew 25:46). Regarding social issues, the Bible provides instruction about the kind of home we should have (Ephesians 5:22-6:4), the relationship that citizens ought to enjoy with their governments (Romans 13:1-7), and how we should treat one another (Matthew 7:12). Thus, Bible is relevant to our lives in all areas.

## Conclusion

The proof for the Bible's inspiration is overwhelming. Whether we are considering fulfilled prophecies, accuracy, unity, the quality of writing or the Bible's relevance, it is obvious that it is the product of God. No wonder the psalmist wrote, "How sweet are Your words to my taste, sweeter than honey to my mouth!" (Psalm 119:103).

## Questions for Consideration

1. What is "scientific foreknowledge"?

2. How does scientific foreknowledge help to prove the inspiration of the Bible?

3. Give an example of a scientific fact revealed in the Bible that you find interesting.

4. In what way has archaeology helped to confirm the Scriptures?

5. How is unity used as a proof for inspiration?

6. Which aspect of the Bible's quality of writing do you think is the most impressive? Why?

7. Should relevance count as a proof for inspiration? Why or why not?

8. Given the evidence for its inspiration, what should our attitude be toward the Bible ?

## Chapter 9

# Jesus Christ: Existence and Identity

Christianity either stands or falls with Jesus. If Jesus' claims to be the Son of God can be substantiated, then all men must obey His will. On the other hand, if His claims can be shown to be mere fabrications, both He and the religion that wears His name ought to be rejected. Either way, the truth is what we must seek. For that reason, we turn our attention to Jesus and examine the available evidence of His existence and His claims.

## The Historical Jesus

Although it is generally granted that Jesus of Nazareth lived during the first century A.D., it is nevertheless important for us to consider the historical evidence that establishes this fact. This evidence can be classified into three separate groups: secular testimony, biblical testimony and circumstantial evidence.

**Secular testimony affirms Jesus' existence.** Perhaps the most famous mention of Jesus Christ found in secular history is in Flavius Josephus' *The Antiquity of the Jews.*

> Now, there was about this time Jesus, a wise man, if it be lawful to call him a man, for he was a doer of wonderful works – a teacher of such men as receive the truth with pleasure. He drew over to him both many of the Jews, and many

of the Gentiles. He was Christ; and when Pilate, at the suggestion of the principle amongst us, had condemned him to the cross, those that loved him at the first did not forsake him, for he appeared to them alive again the third day, as the divine prophets had foretold these and ten thousand other wonderful things concerning him; and the tribe of Christians, so named for him, are not extinct at this day. [1]

To be fair, many question the authenticity of this quotation. Arguing that because the statement "gives expression to a full Christian faith, and since the earliest Christian Fathers who read Josephus do not mention the passage," those who challenge this reference conclude that "it must unhesitatingly be pronounced a Christian interpolation." [2]

Regardless of whether the reasons offered for doubting the quotation's authenticity are convincing,[3] it is not disputed that Josephus, who lived from A.D. 37-100, mentioned Jesus in a later passage. Describing the actions of a man named Ananus, Josephus wrote, "[S]o he assembled the Sanhedrin of judges, and brought before them the brother of Jesus, who was called Christ, whose name was James, and some others; and when he had formed an accusation against them as breakers of the law, he delivered them to be stoned." [4] Even if we granted that the first passage is a forgery, the second passage, although seemingly incidental, would provide evidence that Jesus Christ existed.

Another reference to Jesus in secular works can be found in the writings of the Roman historian Cornelius Tacitus. Born in the mid-first century, Tacitus wrote his history around A.D. 112. In describing the actions of the Roman Emperor Nero, he also provided valuable testimony for the historical Christ:

> But not all the relief that could come from man, not all the bounties that the prince could bestow, nor all the atonements which could be presented to the gods, availed to relieve Nero from the infamy of being believed to have ordered the conflagration, the fire at Rome. Hence, to suppress the rumor, he falsely charged with guilt, and punished with most exquisite tortures, the persons commonly called Christians, who were hated for their enormities. Christus, the founder of the name, was put to death by Pontius Pilate, procura-

tor of Judea in the reign of Tiberius: but the pernicious su-
perstition, repressed for a time broke out again, not only
through Judea, where the mischief originated, but through
the city of Rome also.[5]

Recognizing the value of Tacitus' quotation, F.W. Mattox observed:

> The testimony which is unchallenged historically states that:
> (1) Christ is the founder of the "denomination" of Christians.
> (2) Christ was put to death as a criminal by Pontius Pilate.
> (3) His death took place while Tiberius was Emperor; there-
> fore he must have been born under the reign of Augustus.
> (4) Christianity, this "pernicious superstition," began in Judea
> and was suppressed for a time, then broke out again and
> reached Rome before Tacitus wrote his Annals. (5) Christians
> were persecuted in Rome as early as A.D. 64. (6) "Vast mul-
> titudes" were executed to gratify the "cruelty of one man,"
> Nero. (7) Tacitus recognized they were innocent of the crimes
> charged against them.

> This testimony confirms the facts of the gospels; and, since
> there were large numbers of Christians scattered all over the
> empire as early as 30 years after the death of Christ, the book
> of Acts is also vindicated, and the theories that Christianity
> was a synthesis of the mystery religions or the result of a
> growth of myths must be of necessity forever rejected.[6]

Yet another reference to Christ in a secular work is found in a letter written by a contemporary of Tacitus, Pliny the Younger. Writing
to the Emperor Trajan about the Christians, he observed:

> They also declared that the sum total of their guilt or error
> amounted to no more than this: they had met regularly before
> dawn on a fixed day to chant verses alternately amongst them-
> selves in honor of Christ as if to a god, and also to bind them-
> selves by oath, not for any criminal purpose, but to abstain
> from theft, robbery, and adultery, to commit no breach of trust
> and not to deny a deposit when called upon to restore it.[7]

It is significant to note that none of the three authors mentioned – Josephus, Tacitus or Pliny the Younger – were friendly to Christianity. Yet despite this fact, they all affirmed that a man named Jesus, who was considered by others to be the Christ, lived. When combined with the statements of a number of others we could consider, the evidence from secular testimony overwhelmingly asserts that Jesus of Nazareth lived.

**Biblical testimony affirms Jesus' existence.** In addition to the secular historians who referred to Jesus, the testimony found within the Bible is unanimous regarding His life. Whether it was Peter confessing that Jesus is the Son of God (Matthew 16:16), Thomas professing faith after feeling the scars of the risen Savior (John 20:24-29), or John describing how he had heard, seen and handled the Lord (1 John 1:1), Scripture asserts Jesus' reality without apology. In addition to these and many other passages that could be cited, the beginning of Luke's biography of Jesus is worthy of consideration:

> Inasmuch as many have taken in hand to set in order a narrative of those things which have been fulfilled among us, just as those who from the beginning were eyewitnesses and ministers of the word delivered them to us, it seemed good to me also, having had perfect understanding of all things from the very first, to write to you an orderly account, most excellent Theophilus, that you may know the certainty of those things in which you were instructed (Luke 1:1-4).

Although it is certainly the case that the testimony of the Scriptures must be considered friendly, such does not negate their historical validity. Wayne Jackson makes this clear:

> A.N. Sherwin-White was one of Oxford's premier historians on Roman culture. In his valuable work, *Roman Society and Roman Law in the New Testament* (Grand Rapids: Baker, 1978, p. 186), the professor demonstrated that the Gospels and Acts are much more historically credible than the common works of the Roman world. For example, the New Testament narratives were written by men who were contemporary with the events they recorded. On the other hand, Plutarch's *Lives of the Noble Romans* stands two centuries

from the actual events, and Livy's History of Rome is 500 years this side of its theme. Yet no one doubts the value of these works.

It is readily apparent that the New Testament is not given anything remotely resembling a fair, literary treatment; nevertheless, it passes the credibility-test brilliantly.[8]

Thus, the testimony regarding Jesus that comes from both secular and biblical accounts provides us with the assurance that He lived.

**Circumstantial evidence affirms Jesus' existence.** Although some might find it more impressive to turn to either secular or biblical records to prove the historicity of Christ, it is nevertheless helpful in establishing Jesus' reality to point out several examples of what might be called circumstantial evidence. The first piece of evidence pointing to the existence of Jesus is the way that time is and has been counted for the past two millenniums. The Latin designation *anno domini*, properly abbreviated A.D., literally means, "in the year of the Lord; in the (specified) year since the birth of Christ; in the year of the Christian era." [9] If Jesus never actually walked upon the earth, it seems unlikely that this manner of counting time would have been devised.

A second piece of evidence that points to the reality of Jesus' life is the change in the day of worship from the Old Testament to the New Testament. Under the Law of Moses, individuals worshiped on the Sabbath (Exodus 20:8-11; Leviticus 26:2). The importance that the Jews placed upon keeping the Sabbath day can be seen in the way they dealt with the man who was caught gathering sticks on that day (Numbers 15:32-36). With this zealous behavior in mind, it is truly striking that both the biblical record and historical references show that many of the Jews (as well as other individuals) who lived in the first century changed the day of worship from the seventh day of the week to the first. Interestingly, the practice of worshiping on the first day of the week has continued down through the centuries. But why did such a dramatic change occur? Would such a change have occurred if Jesus never lived? Philip Schaff described the change in this manner:

The day was transferred from the seventh to the first day of the week, not on the ground of a particular command, but by the free spirit of the gospel and by the power of certain great facts which lie at the foundation of the Christian church. It was on that day that Christ rose from the dead; that he appeared to Mary, the disciples of Emmaus, and the assembled apostles; that he poured out his Spirit and founded the church; and that he revealed to his beloved disciple the mysteries of the future. Hence, the first day was already in the apostolic age honorably designated as "the Lord's Day." On that day Paul met with the disciples at Troas and preached till midnight. On that day he ordered the Galatian and Corinthian Christians to make, no doubt in connection with divine service, their weekly contributions to charitable objects according to their ability. It appears, therefore, from the New Testament itself, that Sunday was observed as a day of worship, and in special commemoration of the Resurrection, whereby the work of redemption was finished. [10]

An additional piece of evidence that points to the reality of Jesus is the practice of partaking of the Lord's Supper. Clearly, the very title of this memorial ties it to the existence of Jesus. It is impossible to conceive of the Lord's Supper gaining acceptance if Jesus never actually lived. This is especially true when one considers the instructions for its observation found within the New Testament: "[D]o this ... in remembrance of Me. For as often as you eat this bread and drink this cup, you proclaim the Lord's death till He comes" (1 Corinthians 11:25-26).

## The Identity of Jesus

With a defense of Jesus' historical reality set forth, we now turn our attention to the identity of this man. Who is Jesus? Is He just a carpenter's son from Nazareth? Or is He, as John the Baptizer stated, "The Lamb of God who takes away the sin of the world" (John 1:29)? Ironically, Jesus asked the Pharisees of His day a similar question: "What do you think about the Christ? Whose Son is He?" (Matthew 22:42).

The answers to these questions are, of course, paramount to our study. If it can be shown that Jesus was nothing more than a common man who possessed remarkable leadership skills, then He must take His place alongside the other great leaders throughout history. But if it can be shown that Jesus is more than just a leader, that He is the Son of God, then all men must submit to His will. Thus, Jesus' position of importance would tower above that of any other man who has ever lived. In the remainder of this chapter, we will set forth some of the various claims Jesus made while on earth. The next chapter will deal with whether the claims of Christ can be substantiated.

Students of the New Testament are well aware that Jesus made several claims that deserve to be considered. Interestingly, one of the earliest of these claims was issued by Jesus while He was still a youth. According to Luke's account, Jesus and His family traveled from their home in Nazareth to Jerusalem in order to observe the Passover (Luke 2:41-42). When they were going home, Joseph and Mary realized that Jesus was not with them. Returning to Jerusalem, "they found Him in the temple" (v. 46), and when they inquired about His actions, He responded, "Did you not know that I must be about My Father's business?" (v. 49). Because it is obvious that Jesus was not referring to Joseph's business, He was claiming to be the Son of God.

Other passages find Jesus making a similar claim. After Peter confessed that Jesus was the Son of God, He responded, "Blessed are you, Simon Bar-Jonah, for flesh and blood has not revealed this to you, but My Father who is in heaven" (Matthew 16:17). On the occasion of His trial, the high priest asked, " 'Are You the Christ, the Son of the Blessed?' Jesus said, 'I am' " (Mark 14:61-62). And just before His ascension, Jesus spoke with His apostles and said, "Behold, I send the Promise of My Father upon you; but tarry in the city of Jerusalem until you are endued with power from on high" (Luke 24:49).

Besides claiming to be the Son of God, Jesus also made claims that only a member of the Godhead could make. For example, He claimed to have the power to forgive sins (Mark 2:1-12). Additionally, John's gospel account records the following claims that Jesus made, which if true, show that He is much more than a man. He claimed: "I am the bread of life" (John 6:35); "I am the light of the world" (8:12); "before Abraham was, I AM" (v. 58), "I am the door of the sheep" (10:7); "I am the good shepherd" (v. 11); "I am the resurrection and the life" (11:25); "I am the way, the truth, and the life" (14:6); and "I am the vine, you are the branches" (15:5).

This chart, drawn from an article written by Phil Sanders,[11] contains several other significant claims that Jesus made.

## CLAIMS MADE BY JESUS

- To be the Messiah, the King of the Jews, the Suffering Servant of Isaiah (Matthew 26:63-65; Mark 14:60-62; Luke 22:67-70; John 9:35-37).
- To be the Lord of the Sabbath (Matthew 12:8; Mark 2:28; Luke 6:5).
- To be an appropriate object of religious faith (Matthew 16:15-17; John 5:23; 8:24; 20:28).
- To be the Heir to God (Matthew 28:18).
- To be greater than King David, Solomon, Jonah and the Temple (Matthew 12:3-8; 41-42; Luke 11:31-32).
- To speak eternally binding sayings on His own authority (Matthew 7:24-29; 24:35; John 12:48).
- To be "able" to fulfill the Old Testament scriptures (Matthew 5:17).
- To be the issue upon which eternal destinies depend (John 8:24; 12:48).
- To have exclusive knowledge of the Father and to be the sole source of that knowledge (John 1:18; 14:6-10).
- To be of equal status with the Father and the Spirit and to share "the Name" with them (Matthew 28:19; John 5:18; 10:30).

Jesus' identity cannot be separated from the claims He made. Those claims define Him. If proved true, they warrant obedience; if false, they warrant rejection. In either case, they warrant action. We cannot be neutral about Jesus. Either He is everything, or He is nothing – there is no middle ground. Regardless, we can be certain that He lived and that He made many bold claims. We must now turn our attention to the task of proving those claims to be true.

## Questions for Consideration

1. Why is secular testimony important in proving the existence of Jesus?

2. Why is it significant that individuals not friendly to Christianity confirmed the existence of Jesus and various practices of Christians?

3. Is the Bible a credible historical source? Why?

4. Which piece of circumstantial evidence regarding Jesus' existence do you find most compelling? Why?

5. Why are the claims that Jesus made important?

6. How do the claims made in Jesus' "I am" statements set Him apart from all others?

## Chapter 10

# Jesus Christ: Proving the Claims

Having shown that Jesus of Nazareth actually lived, and having documented several of the claims He made, we now consider whether the claims Jesus made can be substantiated. Is it possible for us to know that Jesus was who He claimed to be? Or must we be content to say that Jesus was an extraordinary man who made remarkable claims?

When all of the evidence is considered, rational individuals can justifiably draw the same conclusion about Jesus Peter did in John 6:68-69: That Jesus had the words of eternal life and that He was indeed the Christ, the Son of the living God.

## Proving the Claims of Jesus

**Jesus' miracles substantiate His claims to be the Son of God.** In a conversation with His apostles just before His death, Jesus said, "Believe Me that I am in the Father and the Father in Me, or else believe Me for the sake of the works themselves" (John 14:11). The works Jesus referred to in this text were the miracles He performed while on earth. Thus, He argued that even if His testimony was rejected, He would still have a witness to His deity – miracles. Peter brought this same fact to the Jews' attention when he preached the first gospel sermon. He argued that Jesus was "a Man attested by God to you by miracles, wonders, and signs which God did through Him in your midst, as you yourselves also know" (Acts

2:22). It was no coincidence that both Jesus and His apostles pointed to the miracles He performed as a proof of His deity.

It is one thing to claim to have performed a miracle – many individuals in our modern age make similar claims. It is, however, quite another thing to prove such a claim. So how can we prove that Jesus worked miracles? First, we must consider the size of the audience for the miracles Jesus performed. Although it is true that Jesus did not always work miracles before large crowds (see Luke 8:51-56), it is just as true that many of His miracles were performed in the presence of great multitudes. Whether it was miraculously feeding the 5,000 (Matthew 14:13-21; Mark 6:30-44; Luke 9:10-17; John 6:1-14), healing the paralytic (Mark 2:1-12), or raising Lazarus from the dead (John 11:38-44), Jesus did not shy away from using His power in the presence of many witnesses. Instead of performing His miracles in hidden locations or only in the company of His closest friends, Jesus' miracles were performed before friends and foes alike.

A second reason for having confidence in Jesus' miraculous ability actually comes from the way His enemies reacted to His works. Over the course of His ministry, their reaction was expressed in four ways: (1) They attributed His power to Satan (Mark 3:20-22); (2) They attempted to deny His involvement (John 9:13-34); (3) They ignored His power (Mark 6:1-6); and (4) They sought to conceal the evidence of His divinity (John 12:9-11). Despite these various reactions, the enemies of Jesus could not deny that miracles had taken place. Thus, their acknowledgements of demons cast out, of a blind man made to see, of sick people made well, and of a dead man brought back to life provide a strong reason for us to believe in the miracles of Jesus.

Third, our confidence in the miraculous abilities of Jesus is strengthened when we consider that His miracles are reported, in many cases, by more than one author. Consequently, rather than trusting the testimony of just one individual, readers of the New Testament can take some comfort in noting that many of the miracles of Jesus are set forth and affirmed in more than one of the gospel accounts. Eric Lyons and Kyle Butt explained the significance of this fact:

> Unlike Islam and Mormonism, each of which relies upon
> the accounts/writings of one alleged inspired man (Muham-

mad and Joseph Smith, respectively), Christianity rests upon the foundation of multiple writers. Consider also that certain miracles Jesus performed, specifically the feeding of the 5,000 and His resurrection, are recorded in all four gospel accounts. Furthermore, the writers' attestation of Jesus' life and miracles is similar enough so as not to be contradictory, but varied enough so that one cannot reasonably conclude that they participated in collusion in order to perpetrate a hoax. Truly, the fact that multiple writers attest to the factuality of Jesus' miracles should not be taken lightly and dismissed with the wave of the hand. [1]

A fourth reason for placing confidence in the miracles of Jesus is found when we consider the kinds of miracles He worked. One could hardly argue that Jesus' miracles were nothing more than trickery or the sleight of hand. Unlike so many today who claim to be able to perform miracles, the miracles Jesus performed left little room for doubt. Who could question that a man, blind from birth, had received his sight in any way other than a miracle? Who could question that a man, dead for four days, was brought back to life other than by the miraculous power of Jesus? The truth is that the miracles Jesus performed were subject to sensory perception. The water that He turned into wine could be tasted (John 2:7-10) and Malchus' restored ear could be seen (Luke 22:49-51). If nothing else, it lends credibility to Jesus' miracles.

Finally, it is striking for us to consider that the miracles of Jesus defy natural explanation. Fish and loaves do not naturally multiply themselves in a matter of moments, yet 5,000 people were reportedly fed from only five loaves and two fish (Matthew 14:17). The dead do not suddenly arise from their tombs, yet Lazarus came forth, "bound hand and foot with graveclothes" (John 11:44) – an event that even the enemies of Jesus did not deny! How do we explain these events and so many others like them? The only explanation is to say that they occurred as a result of the miraculous abilities of Jesus.

To say that the miracles of Jesus provide us with a reason to believe in His deity would be an understatement. The value of His miracles cannot be overestimated. R.C. Trench made this point quite clear when he described the void that a lack of miracles would leave behind:

Our loss would be irreparable, if they were absent from our sacred history, if we could not point to them there. It is not too much to say that this absence would be fatal. There are indeed two miracles, that of the Incarnation and that of the Resurrection, round which the whole scheme of redemption revolves, and without which it would cease to be a redemptive scheme at all. But we are speaking here not of miracles whereof Christ was the subject, but of those which he wrought; and of them too we affirm that they long belong to the very idea of a Redeemer, which would remain altogether incomplete without them. [2]

Clearly, the miracles of Jesus confirm His identity as the Son of God. **Jesus' birth and resurrection substantiate His claims to be the Son of God.** If anything about the life of Jesus catches one's attention, it would be the biblical accounts of His birth and His resurrection. Both events sustain His claims to be divine.

Two important facts to consider about Jesus' birth: it was to be miraculous in nature – predicted by the prophet Isaiah some 700 years before it transpired (Isaiah 7:14). Also, the place of His birth was foretold by the prophet Micah (Micah 5:2), making the biblical record of Jesus' birth very striking.

Wayne Jackson also observed how striking it is to consider how the genealogical records found in the New Testament support the virgin birth:

In listing the "legal" genealogy of Christ from Abraham to Joseph, Matthew used the term "begat" no less than 39 times. Yet, when he came to Jesus, the word is conspicuously dropped from his vocabulary. He simply says, "… Joseph was the husband of Mary, of whom was born Jesus, who is called the Christ." (Matt. 1:16). This is a carefully worded testimony to the virgin birth. Luke also, in a guarded statement, notes that Jesus was the son "as was supposed" of Joseph. (Luke 3:23). [3]

Jackson also showed how the virgin birth related to the death of Jesus:

Because of His confession that He was the Son of God, Christ was judged worthy of death. The issue is clear. If

Jesus was not the Son of God in a unique way, He was guilty of blasphemy and thus deserving of death according to the Old Testament law (Lev. 24:16). It therefore would seem that a denial of the virgin birth of Christ is an affirmation that His death was just! [4]

In other words, if Jesus was not born of a virgin, He deserved to die. But if He was the virgin-born Christ, then His death was truly undeserved (see 2 Corinthians 5:21).

Like His birth, the account of Jesus' resurrection proves critical when one questions His deity. In fact, if it can be shown that Jesus arose from the dead, all the questions about His identity will vanish. [5] In view of the resurrection's importance, certain facts must be considered: Jesus predicted His resurrection (Luke 18:31-33); Jesus' enemies made provisions to guard His tomb (Matthew 27:62-66); it was widely reported and is still granted that the tomb of Jesus became empty on or by the Sunday after His crucifixion (Luke 24:17-24); the enemies of Jesus never denied that His tomb was empty (Matthew 28:11-15); the followers of Christ exhibited a newfound courage and became willing to proclaim His resurrection, despite threats to their lives (Acts 5:27-32); and numerous witnesses claimed to have seen Jesus after His resurrection (1 Corinthians 15:3-8). Truly, if Jesus arose from the dead, He was who He claimed to be – the Son of God.

**Jesus' life and influence substantiate His claims to be the Son of God.** Despite whatever else might be said about Jesus, His influence, which came as a result of His life and teaching, has been as great, if not greater, than that of any other figure to live upon the earth. His greatness began with the purity of His life. Described in Scripture as a "lamb without blemish and without spot" (1 Peter 1:19), Jesus truly lived a sinless life (Hebrews 4:15; 1 Peter 2:22). Philip Schaff wrote:

> In vain do we look through the entire biography of Jesus for a single stain or the slightest shadow on his moral character. There never lived a more harmless being on earth. He injured nobody, he took advantage of nobody. He never spoke an improper word, he never committed a wrong action. [6]

When the Jews sought some error to charge Jesus with, they were able to find only two liars who could agree on His crime. Matthew described this telling event:

> Now the chief priests, the elders, and all the council sought false testimony against Jesus to put Him to death, but found none. Even though many false witnesses came forward, they found none. But at last two false witnesses came forward and said, "This fellow said, 'I am able to destroy the temple of God and to build it in three days.'" And the high priest arose and said to Him, "Do You answer nothing? What is it these men testify against You?" But Jesus kept silent. And the high priest answered and said to Him, "I put You under oath by the living God: Tell us if You are the Christ, the Son of God!" Jesus said to him, "It is as you said. Nevertheless, I say to you, hereafter you will see the Son of Man sitting at the right hand of the Power, and coming on the clouds of heaven." Then the high priest tore his clothes, saying, "He has spoken blasphemy! What further need do we have of witnesses? Look, now you have heard His blasphemy! What do you think?" They answered and said, "He is deserving of death" (Matthew 26:59-66).

Adding weight to the claims that Jesus made while on earth is the vast influence He has exerted upon untold numbers of individuals. Describing this influence, Philip Schaff wrote:

> [T]his Jesus of Nazareth, without money and arms, conquered more millions than Alexander, Caesar, Mohammed, and Napoleon; without science and learning, he shed more light on things human and divine than all philosophers and scholars combined; without the eloquence of schools, he spoke such words of life as were never spoken before or since, and produced effects which lie beyond the reach of orator or poet; without writing a single line, he set more pens in motion, and furnished themes for more sermons, orations, discussions, learned volumes, works of art, and songs of praise, than the whole army of great men of ancient and modern times. [7]

Bernard Ramm's description of Jesus' influence is also noteworthy:

> Whether Jesus be a man or God, whether the gospels be
> mainly fiction or fancy, certainly a historic person named
> Jesus gave certain men such an impact as to be unequaled
> by far in the entire annals of the human race. After nearly
> two thousand years the impact is not at all spent, but daily
> there are people who have tremendous revolutionary ex-
> periences which they associate with Jesus Christ, be He dead
> or risen in heaven. The personality of Jesus is without par-
> allel. It is unique and incomparable. [8]

Could a man who made so many significant claims, whose actions
were not performed in a corner but in the public arena, whose manner
of life and teachings were severely scrutinized, yet who still maintained
the ability to influence men to live lives of self-denial (see Matthew 16:24)
have been anything other than genuine? To argue that Jesus was a de-
ceiver, one must be prepared to question the rationality of the millions
who have believed His claims. [9] In addition, one must be able to provide
adequate natural explanations for the miracles He reportedly performed
while explaining away all the other supernatural facts, especially those
surrounding His birth and resurrection, associated with Him. When such
hurdles are cleared, one must also repudiate the numerous passages found
within the Bible that proclaim Jesus to be the Christ. The task will require the critic to provide convincing reasons as to why those testimonies,
written within a few years of Jesus' life, ought to be disregarded. This
task simply cannot be done!

## Liar, Lunatic or Lord?

How must we view Jesus of Nazareth? Was He merely a great moral
teacher? Was He a motivator of men? Or was He more? C.S. Lewis
made very clear what our options actually are:

> I am trying here to prevent anyone from saying the really
> foolish thing that people often say about Him: "I'm ready
> to accept Jesus as a great moral teacher, but I don't accept
> His claim to be God." That is the one thing we must not say.
> A man who was merely a man and said the sort of things

Jesus said would not be a great moral teacher. He would either be a lunatic – on a level with the man who says he is a poached egg – or else he would be the Devil of Hell. You must make your choice. Either this man was, and is, the Son of God: or else a madman or something worse. You can shut Him up for a fool, you can spit at Him and kill Him as a demon; or you can fall at His feet and call Him Lord and God. But let us not come with any patronizing nonsense about His being a great human teacher. He has not left that open to us. He did not intend to. [10]

When we consider that Jesus used His intellectual ability to silence the critics of His day on more than one occasion (Matthew 22:15-46; Luke 20:1-8), it seems clear that He had full possession of His mental faculties and was not a lunatic. When we consider that He willingly accepted the sentence of death handed down to Him (John 19:10-11; Isaiah 53:7-9), we may rightly suppose that He did not die merely to propagate a lie. The only conclusion that we can draw is that Jesus is truly the Lord – the very Son of God.

## Questions for Consideration

1. What do you consider to be the strongest proof for the claims Jesus made?

2. What is the most compelling reason to believe in the miracles of Jesus?

3. Why is the way Jesus' enemies viewed His miracles significant?

4. Why are the accounts of Jesus' birth and resurrection important to His deity?

5. What does the influence of Jesus say about the kind of life He lived?

6. Reread the quotation from C.S. Lewis. Do you believe that Lewis properly assessed how Jesus must be viewed? Why or why not?

## Chapter 11

# The Origin
# of Man

The world where we live lends itself to verification. We can record the precision of its various aspects; we can perform tests upon it. For these reasons and many others, rational individuals cannot deny that the universe where they dwell exists. Commenting upon this fact, Wilbur M. Smith, in his valuable work *Therefore Stand*, wrote:

> That we live in a universe made up of a vast number of innumerable bodies, dominated by inexorable laws of what we call nature, a universe that can be seen and handled, studied, and in part understood, embracing both organic matter and organic objects, which we call living, is of course at the very foundation of anything called sane thinking. [1]

But once it is admitted that the universe exists, another question naturally follows. Smith continued, "Acknowledging the present existence of this universe, we cannot escape, in mature life, coming face to face with an inevitable question: How did this universe come into existence?" [2] Putting the question into another form, we ask, "From whence comes man?" The purpose of this chapter is to explore the possible answers that might be offered in response to this question and draw the conclusion the evidence warrants.

So what possible solutions could be cited to answer the question of man's origin? In truth, only three possibilities exist: man and the universe have always existed; man and the universe came into existence by the means of an evolutionary process; or man and the universe were created by a supernatural power. If two of these three can be proved false, the third must be accepted as true.

Neither theists nor those who reject the existence of God take seriously the first option. Instead, it is generally granted that the universe must have come into existence at some point in time. This belief is, in part, based on our understanding of the second law of thermodynamics. Dr. Henry M. Morris explains:

> The second law of thermodynamics states that in any real process or system in which energy is being transferred into other forms, at least some of it is transformed into heat energy which cannot be converted back into other useful forms. That is, although none of the energy is destroyed, some of it deteriorates and becomes less useful and available for work than it was at the beginning of the process ...

> ... this law implies that there is a continual decrease of useful energy for performing the work of running the universe or, in other terms, that there is a continual increase of disorder in the universe. The universe is therefore growing old, wearing out running down, due ultimately to burn itself out when all of its useful energy is converted to unavailable heat energy and the entire universe reaches a constant uniform, low temperature, and ceases all its motions.[3]

In essence, if our universe is in the process of running down as the second law of thermodynamics indicates, the universe simply could not have existed eternally. Otherwise, it would have already ceased to exist. So with the idea of eternal existence cast aside, we must now turn our attention to the second alternative – evolution.

## Evolution

**What does "evolution" mean?** Because the word "evolution" can be used in a variety of ways, understanding its meaning within the context of its use is vital. In his article "The Theory of Evolution: A Philosophic Problem," James D. Bales noted five different uses of the term:

> First, evolution describes the invention and development of a product. We speak of the evolution of the wheel, the battleship, and the airplane. These things were not the nonplanned product of the blind movements of matter … .

> Second, we speak of the evolution of the egg into the chicken and the seed into the plant … . This evolution is the unfolding of that which is latent within the seed; one starts with a seed which has life in itself, the unfolding is within certain limits, and there is scientific proof that the life cycle of the seed is a reality.

> Third, limited variation within the groups has also been called evolution. There are varieties of dogs, and there are small horses and there are large horses … . In all such cases we start with life, the seed produces after its basic kind, and there is a limit to the variations.

> Fourth, theistic evolution is the term used by some to describe evolution as God's method of creation. Some theistic evolutionists call in God to bridge certain gaps. The consistent evolutionist, however, is as willing to call in God a dozen times as he is one time. He is not willing to call in God at all, and he does not consider the theistic evolutionists as any more scientific than he considers the creationist … .

> Fifth, evolution is the word which also describes the total explanation of life's origin and manifold forms. This General Theory of Evolution … maintains that our universe, our solar system, our earth, and life and its manifold forms, have become what they are as the result of natural forces, without any intelligent direction, acting on matter. [4]

With those basic designations before us, it is obvious that the general theory of evolution and its subsidiary, theistic evolution, are the uses we must focus upon.

**What is evolution?** The evolutionary process has been described in many ways. One description, written by Theodosius Dobzhasky, aptly defines the theory:

> The theory of evolution asserts that (1) the beings now living have descended from different beings which lived in the past; (2) the evolutionary changes were more or less gradual, so that if we could assemble all the individuals which have ever inhabited the earth, a fairly continuous array of forms would emerge; (3) the changes were predominantly divergent, so that the ancestors of the now living forms were on the whole different from each other than these forms themselves are; (4) all these changes have arisen from causes which now continue to be in operation, and which therefore can be studied experimentally. [5]

Upon reading this description, one can see that several assumptions are involved within the theory. G.A. Kerkut listed seven assumptions basic to the evolutionary process:

1. The first assumption is that non-living things gave rise to living matter, i.e., spontaneous generation occurred.

2. The second assumption is that spontaneous generation occurred only once.

The other assumptions all follow the second one.

3. The third assumption is that the viruses, bacteria, plants and animals are all interrelated.

4. The fourth assumption is that the protozoa gave rise to the metazoa.

5. The fifth assumption is that the various invertebrate phyla are interrelated.

6. The sixth assumption is that the invertebrates gave rise to the vertebrates.

7. The seventh assumption is that within the vertebrates the fish gave rise to the amphibia, the amphibia to the reptiles, and the reptiles to the birds and mammals. Sometimes this

is expressed in other words, i.e., that the modern amphibia and reptiles had a common ancestral stock, and so on. [6]

Variations of the evolutionary theory can be traced back to the ancient Greeks. One early promoter was Anaximander (c. 610-545 B.C.). Frederick Copleston described Anaximander's views:

> Anaximander makes a clear guess as to the origin of man. "… he further says that in the beginning man was born from animals of another species, for while other animals quickly find nourishment for themselves, man alone needs a lengthy period of suckling, so that had he been originally as he is now, he could never have survived." [7]

Copleston notes that Anaximander "does not explain – a perennial difficulty for evolutionists – how man survived this transition stage." [8] Despite the efforts of the early Greeks and others who followed, the theory of evolution did not gain a major foothold among prominent thinkers until Charles Darwin published, *On the Origin of the Species* in 1859. Darwin proposed the three components that are needed for evolution to occur: massive replication, variation and a selection mechanism. By employing these three components, Neil A. Manson describes Darwin's theory as asserting that "nature creates the appearance of intelligence (in the form of extremely well-adapted organisms) by massive reproduction, genetic variation, and natural selection." [9] Thus, evolutionists conclude, "Organisms will look like they were designed by an extremely intelligent designer, but the appearance masks reality." [10]

**What are some problems with the theory of evolution?** Having set forth the theory of evolution and described how its proponents say it works, we need to examine some of its basic problems. One problem with the theory of evolution is that science is unable to account for dead matter producing living matter. Oliver Lodge described this problem:

> [Science] has not yet witnessed the origin of the smallest trace of life from dead matter; all life, so far as has been watched, proceeds from antecedent life … . The law of evolution not only studies change and progress, it seeks to trace sequences back to antecedents; it strains after the origin of all things. But ultimate origins are inscrutable. [11]

In essence, the first essential step of evolution, the production of living matter from non-living matter has never been observed.

A second problem with the theory of evolution can be found, ironically, in one of pieces of evidence that evolutionists claim supports the theory – the fossil record. This problem is twofold. First, the fossil records do not show the transitional forms of animals that would have certainly been present given the massive replication evolution requires. Dr. Austin H. Clark wrote:

> No matter how far back we go in the fossil records of previous animal life upon the earth we find no trace of any animal forms which are intermediate between various major groups of phyla ... . The greatest groups of animal life do not merge into one another. They are and have been fixed from the beginning ... . No animals are known even from the earliest rocks which cannot at once be assigned to their proper phylum or major group ... .[12]

Although Clark's conclusions were written almost a century ago, they maintain their validity. Brad Harrub and Bert Thompson, in their book, *The Truth About Human Origins*, make a similar point:

> Of all the branches to be found on that infamous "evolutionary tree of life," the one leading to man should be the best documented. After all, as the most recent evolutionary arrival, pre-human fossils supposedly would have been exposed to natural decay processes for the shortest length of time, and thus should be better preserved and easier to find than others ... . In addition, since hominid fossils are of the greatest interest to man (because they are supposed to represent his past), it is safe to say that more people have been searching for them longer than for any other type of fossils. If there are any real transitional forms anywhere in the world, they should be documented most abundantly in the line leading from the first primate to modern man.[13]

The second problem with the fossil record lies in the use of single artifacts. Often a single bone will be used to construct what evolutionists conceive as the missing link in the evolutionary chain. Such action, however, lacks justification. Harrub and Thompson noted:

> More than 6,000 human-like fossils exist. Some are partial skulls, while others may be only a few teeth. Most of these fossils can be placed into one of two groups: apes or humans. A few fossils do have odd characteristics or show abnormal bone structure. But does this mean that humans evolved? No. It simply means that we have variations in bone structure – variations you probably can see all around you. Some heads are big; others are small. Some noses are pointed, and some are flat. Some jawbones look angled, while some look square. Does this mean some of us are still "evolving"? Or does it mean that there are occasional differences in humans? [14]

Third, the theory of evolution fails to provide an adequate explanation as to how man developed free will. Richard Holt Hutton wrote:

> Neither the scientific principle of what called the "correlation of forces," nor the Darwinian law of selection, seems to throw the slightest glimpse of light on the origin of human free-will, and that sense of responsibility of which free-will is the absolute condition. As for the Darwinian law, it is simply inconceivable, supposing you deny free-will to the lower types of organic beings, out of which, on his conception, the higher species are gradually elaborated by natural selection, that an accidental variation should introduce free-will. [15]

It is truly inconceivable that man's sense of moral obligation, which exists in conjunction with his free will, resulted by pure chance.

Finally, the variations and mutations that evolutionists depend so much upon are unsuited to produce what the theory of evolution requires. Wayne Jackson addressed this point:

> A mutation is simply a change in the genetic structure of an organism. No one knows exactly what causes the changes in nature though they may be induced artificially by radia-

tion, chemicals, etc. That these changes occur within limits is undeniable; what is denied is that mutations can precipitate sufficient change for the formation of a new "kind" of animal, and this is what the evolutionary speculation requires. Here are some facts regarding mutations.

(1) They occur very rarely; "perhaps once in a million animals or once in a million lifetimes." (*Science Today*, Chapter by C.H. Waddington, p. 36.)

(2) They are destructive. "Most mutations are bad, in fact good ones are so rare that we may consider them all as bad." (H.J. Muller, *Time*, November 11, 1946, p. 96.)

(3) Mutations are unable to create anything; they only change existing structures. "A fact that has been obvious for many years is that Mendelian mutations deal only with changes in existing characteristics, never with the appearance of a new functioning character." (H. Graham Cannon, *The Evolution of Living Things*, p. 92.) Dr. Richard Goldschmidt catalogued a number of structures which he claimed could not possibly have developed by means of mutations. Among them are hair, teeth, feathers, blood circulation, nerves and compound eyes. (The Material Basis of Evolution, pp. 6-7). [16]

## Creation

Having dismissed the theory of evolution as unacceptable, the only alternative that remains regarding man's origin is to say that he was created by a supernatural power. This idea, of course, is affirmed throughout the Bible. In fact, the Bible begins with that assertion: "In the beginning God created the heavens and the earth" (Genesis 1:1). Regarding this passage, Wilbur Smith contends:

The first chapter of Genesis is placed at the beginning of our Bible, (1) to show mankind that the world in which he lives originally proceeded from the creative activity of God; (2) that God alone, the one true God, is the creator of the world; (3) that in creating the world He reveals Himself to be the eternal God, of omnipotence, omniscience, and infinite goodness; and (4) finally to inform man of the noble origin of the human species, and of the exalted dignity which must ever attach to the human race, because of the fact that man was originally made in the image of God.[17]

It should be remembered that the creation account is upheld, rather than disregarded, throughout the rest of the Bible. For example, Jesus rebuked the Jews of His day and asked, "Have you not read that He who made them at the beginning 'made them male and female,' and said, 'For this reason a man shall leave his father and mother and be joined to his wife, and the two shall become one flesh'?" (Matthew 19:4-5). In addition, passages like Colossians 1:16-17 and Hebrews 1:2 affirm the creation by detailing the work that the Son accomplished at that time. Likewise, the Bible affirms that the world was created out of nothing. The psalmist affirmed this truth in Psalm 33:6: "By the word of the Lord the heavens were made, and all the host of them by the breath of His mouth." The author of Hebrews also confirmed this truth: "By faith we understand that the worlds were framed by the word of God, so that the things which are seen were not made of things which are visible" (11:3). Obviously, many other passages could be cited, including God's defense before Job: "Where were you when I laid the foundations of the earth?" (Job 38:4). Nevertheless, it is sufficient to say that the Bible asserts the creation account. For this reason, the various positions that seek to combine creation and evolution – theistic evolution, the day-age theory, the gap theory, et al. – must be rejected in view of Scripture. The significance of this fact, Smith notes, is felt when one considers "that for two thousand years men have felt it necessary to consider this ancient Hebrew record [Genesis 1] when discussing the subject of creation."[18]

Objections to the creation account often focus upon a supposed time discrepancy. Critics claim that dating methods now currently used are able to show conclusively that the fossil records are much older than the time frame allowed by Scripture. Because of this charge, some creationists have developed theories designed to resolve this conflict. The Day-Age theory, for example, asserts the days of Genesis 1 were not literal 24-hour periods of time. Instead, the theory goes, they potentially spanned millions of years. Such an assertion, however, fails to recognize that Exodus 20:11 ties the length of the days of creation to that of the Sabbath – certainly a literal 24-hour day. In that passage Moses wrote: "For in six days the Lord made the heavens and the earth, the sea, and all that is in them, and rested the seventh day. Therefore the Lord blessed the Sabbath day and hallowed it." So with that theory cast aside, how can an individual who takes the Bible literally account for the alleged time discrepancies? Foy L. Kirkpatrick offers this answer:

> It is true that the Bible believer cannot match every rock and layer with a verse in Genesis, but there seems to be enough latitude in both the reading of the rocks and in the reading of the record to harmonize the two without difficulty. If one begins with a perfectly aged earth, which was completely renovated by a devastating flood, the Christian has an explanation for the earth that is consistent with observed conditions today. He does not need to imagine vast periods of time for either evolution or geology, and he does not need to reconcile the Bible with geology. [19]

## The Only Option

The significance of man's origin is obvious. If man is created, he owes his allegiance to his creator. But if he is simply the result of billions of years of trial and error, his position at the top of the evolutionary chain is certainly precarious. The truth of the matter, however, is that evolution is not an established fact; instead, it remains an unproven theory. [20] Because of this, creation stands as the only available option that adequately answers the question: From whence comes man?

No doubt contemplating this, Augustine (354-430) wrote:

> I asked the earth; and it answered, "I am not He;" and whatsoever are therein made the same confession. I asked the sea and the deeps, and the creeping things that lived, and they replied, "We are not thy God, seek higher than we." I asked the breezy air, and the universal air with its inhabitants answered, "Anaximenes was deceived, I am not God." I asked the heavens, the sun, moon, and stars: "Neither," say

they, "are we the God whom thou seekest." And I answered unto all these things which stand about the door of my flesh, "Ye have told me concerning my God, that ye are not He; tell me something about Him." And with a loud voice they exclaimed, "He made us." [21]

We would do well to take heed to the admonition of Peter, who wrote, "Therefore let those who suffer according to the will of God commit their souls to Him in doing good, as to a faithful Creator" (1 Peter 4:19). Truly, God is the Creator of all!

## Questions for Consideration

1. What are the possible ways one can account for man's origin?

2. Why is the possibility of eternal existence not acceptable?

3. How would you describe the theory of evolution?

4. What do you consider the strongest argument against evolution?

5. Why is Genesis 1 such an important chapter?

6. How do other passages in the Bible support the creation account?

7. How can a creationist account for the alleged time discrepancies associated with the biblical account?

8. Why must the Day-Age theory be rejected?

## Chapter 12

# Common Questions Answered

When any topic is carefully studied, certain questions must be answered. Some of these questions are foundational in nature and require immediate attention. Other questions, however, tend to spring up as individuals wrestle with new or complex ideas. Although these auxiliary questions are not as urgent, they are nevertheless legitimate and demand to be answered. The intention of this chapter is to answer four questions commonly asked by those who study Christian evidences.

## A Question About God

As individuals consider the question of God's existence, the classical arguments – the cosmological argument, the teleological argument, the ontological argument, and the moral argument – are generally set forth. Upon careful examination of these arguments, it is not unusual for individuals to accept the conclusions that the arguments seek to establish, i.e., that there must be a first cause, a designer, a lawgiver, etc. But even if these arguments are accepted as valid, the question that is often, and rightly, asked is: How do these arguments lead us to believe in the God described in the Bible?

Those who reason in this manner are correct to recognize that just because there must be a first cause (as per the cosmological argument), it does not necessarily follow that the first cause is benevolent. This recognition leads to what is known as the identification problem. Neil A. Manson explains this problem:

> Why are we entitled to assume that the first, uncaused cause (whoever or whatever that is) is God? No reason has been given for thinking that any being that is a first, uncaused cause must also be all the other things that God is supposed to be: omnipotent, omniscient, morally perfect, and so on.[1]

So how is this problem solved? First, we must have a clear idea of the identity of the God we are seeking to prove. God's identity, set forth in Scripture, is composed of the attributes of omnipotence, omniscience and omni-benevolence.[2] Although one might grant that the cosmological argument does not, by itself, point to the existence of a being that indisputably possesses all three of these attributes, it does imply that the first cause – by virtue of its power to create the things in existence – is omnipotent. Omniscience is also seemingly an attribute of a being that creates all others because a maker must have knowledge of what is made.

When we combine this fact with the implication of the teleological argument – that the designer of the universe is omniscient – and that of the moral argument – that the lawgiver is omni-benevolent – we find that the classical arguments do indeed point to the God of the Bible. When used collectively, the classical arguments for God's existence answer the identity problem.

It also bears noting that if the ontological argument is true, there is no identity problem whatsoever. This, of course, is the case because the argument depends upon the assertion that God is the greatest conceivable being. As such, God must possess all of the various attributes ascribed to Him in the Bible to the fullest extent.

## A Question About the Bible

Any study that seeks to uphold the truthfulness of the Bible must be prepared to answer questions about the various events that are reported therein. One event that is commonly called into question is the flood of Noah's day (see Genesis 6-8). Regarding this event, the following questions are often asked: (1) Was the flood local or universal? and (2) Was the ark large enough to accommodate the various kinds of animals that God commanded Noah to preserve?

To answer the first question, we must turn our attention to the text itself. Regardless of whatever else might be said, the assertion of the Bible must not be dismissed. So what does the text say? First, the text provides us with some insight when we consider God's reason for sending the flood: God looked upon the earth, and indeed it was corrupt; for all flesh had corrupted their way on the earth. And God said to Noah, "The end of all flesh has come before Me, for the earth is filled with violence through them; and behold, I will destroy them with the earth" (Genesis 6:12-13).

If these verses point to anything, they point to a global, and not a local, punishment. Such a conclusion can be drawn when we notice the emphasis that is placed on "all flesh."

Additionally, the actual account of the flood points to a global destruction:

> And the waters prevailed exceedingly on the earth, and all the high hills under the whole heaven were covered. The waters prevailed fifteen cubits upward, and the mountains were covered. And all flesh died that moved on the earth: birds and cattle and beasts and every creeping thing that creeps on the earth, and every man. All in whose nostrils was the breath of the spirit of life, all that was on the dry land, died. So He destroyed all living things which were on the face of the ground: both man and cattle, creeping thing and bird of the air. They were destroyed from the earth. Only Noah and those who were with him in the ark remained alive. And the waters prevailed on the earth one hundred and fifty days (Genesis 7:1-24).

Likewise, when it is remembered that the ark came to rest on the mountains of Ararat (Genesis 8:4), mountains that exceed 16,000 feet in height, and that water seeks its own level, it seems ridiculous to conclude that such a volume of water could have been contained in a local area. Emphasizing this point, H.C. Leupold concludes, "[A] flood of more than 16,000 feet, that is to say, of more than three miles in depth could not be confined to any portion of the earth but must necessarily spread itself out over the entire earth's surface."[3]

What about the size of the ark? Is it plausible to believe that Noah's ark was able to carry every kind of animal along with the food necessary to provide for such a load? To answer this, we must actually answer two separate questions: (1) How many animals did Noah have to carry on the ark? and (2) What was the actual size of Noah's ark?

So how many animals did Noah have to carry on the ark? The text of Genesis answers:

> And of every living thing of all flesh you shall bring two of every sort into the ark, to keep them alive with you; they shall be male and female. Of the birds after their kind, of animals after their kind, and of every creeping thing of the earth after its kind, two of every kind will come to you to keep them alive (6:19-20).

Pointing out the significance of this passage, Harry Rimmer, in *The Harmony of Science and Scripture*, wrote, "Noah was not under the necessity of finding room in his ark for every variety and specimen of animal and bird alive today. As soon as we see this, the problem of the ark is simplified tremendously. The specific command is 'of each kind.' " [4]

D.R. Dungan's answer also proves helpful:

> [I]t must be remembered that the great majority of the animals were small; and even the larger species of animals may have been young, and needed but a small amount of space or food either, while the great amount of all these species were birds, and small birds at that.[5]

We must now determine the actual size of Noah's ark. Because the dimensions set forth in the Bible are in cubits – 300 in length, 50 in width and 30 in height (Genesis 6:15) – and because we are unsure as to the exact length of the ancient cubit, we are left to speculate as to the actual size of the ark. Nevertheless, if we assume that a cubit is approximately eighteen inches, the dimensions of the ark would be enormous – 450 feet long, 75 feet wide and 45 feet high. Even at this conservative estimate, there would be ample room in the ark for the cargo the Scriptures demand. Regarding this, Warren Wilcox noted:

> Noah's cubit may have been as much as 24 inches. If so, the ark would have been 600 feet long, 100 feet wide, and 60 feet

high with 3,600,000 cubic feet of space. This is the equivalent of the cubic feet of 1,342 cattle cars each just larger than 40x8x8. Again, all 35,000 necessary species (not kinds) would need only 100 cattle cars to hold them (the average size of all animals is that of a cat – of course, a certain number would be much larger and require more room, but most are smaller and require very little room – fleas could easily find a convenient dog to live on). This would leave the equivalent space of 1,242 cattle cars for food and Noah's family.[6]

The truth is that the ark described in Scripture would have been well suited to sustain the payload assigned to it. It must also be remembered that many aspects of such a flood could never be explained apart from the hand of God. As we consider questions about the flood of Noah, we must never do so without acknowledging God's role.

## What About Dinosaurs?
The evidence that dinosaurs once lived upon the earth cannot be denied. Whether one considers the many fossils that have been discovered, the ancient artifacts that depict such creatures, or even ancient historical testimony,[7] the evidence for their existence is overwhelming. Despite this evidence, many religious people have equated the existence of dinosaurs with the theory of evolution, which claims that dinosaurs became extinct more than 70 million years before man lived.[8] Thus, a discussion of dinosaurs has often been shunned.

So what about the dinosaurs? If dinosaurs ever lived upon the earth, they must have been created during the same week as man. Making this point, Exodus 20:11 states, "For in six days the Lord made the heavens and the earth, the sea, and all that is in them, and rested the seventh day. Therefore the Lord blessed the Sabbath day and hallowed it." Such a fact is also substantiated by the notable passage found in Job 40:15-24. That text describes an animal known simply as "behemoth" (v. 15). This mighty animal, which had a "tail like a cedar" (v. 17), was "the first of the ways of God; only He who made him can bring near His sword" (v. 19). Given this description, it seems that the "behemoth" was most likely a dinosaur.

Several passages in the King James Version of the Bible use the word "dragon" to describe the ancient creatures. For example, Psalm 148:7 states, "Praise the Lord from the earth, ye dragons and all deeps." Rather than seeking to conjure up images of fire-breathing monsters, the word "dragon" in these passages points to an animal that lived upon the earth. It seems at least reasonable to conclude that this creature could have been a dinosaur.

But how could dinosaurs and men coexist? This question fails to consider that many of the largest dinosaurs were herbivores and not carnivores. Thus, these plant-eating giants would have been much less fierce than their fellow creatures. Additionally, it also fails to consider the ability that men have to conquer and even train the most dangerous of animals. From lions, tigers and bears, to elephants and killer whales, men have captured and trained numerous animals. Knowing this, we should not assume that man would have been incapable of doing so even to the most vicious of the dinosaurs. In fact, God charged Adam with this responsibility from the beginning:

> So God created man in His own image; in the image of God He created him; male and female He created them. Then God blessed them, and God said to them, "Be fruitful and multiply; fill the earth and subdue it; have dominion over the fish of the sea, over the birds of the air, and over every living thing that moves on the earth" (Genesis 1:27-28).

Finally, although it is only speculation, we have good reasons to believe that the results of the flood might have accelerated the extinction of the dinosaurs. Kyle Butt and Eric Lyons discuss this possibility:

> So why did dinosaurs eventually become extinct if some did survive the Flood? One reason may be that the dinosaurs which survived the Flood on Noah's ark were not able to cope very well in the new world, because the climate was so different. One indication that the world was very different after the Flood comes from an understanding of how the ages of people at their deaths decreased by hundreds of years. [9]

Given the dramatic climate change that would undoubtedly result from a global flood, it is certainly reasonable to conclude that such would have dramatically affected the dinosaurs. To what extent this climate change would have affected them, however, remains unknown. Regardless, we need not fear the claims of the evolutionists regarding dinosaurs.

## A Question About Miracles

Because the Bible is filled with examples of miracles and because most of the evidence with respect to Jesus' deity is tied to the miraculous, it is not unreasonable for an individual to question whether miracles occur today. After all, if Christians must believe that various miracles occurred in the past, why should they not believe that miraculous events still occur? To answer this, we must turn our attention to Scripture. In particular, we must consider what Scripture says about the purpose and the duration of miracles.

With regard to the purpose of miracles, the Bible plainly asserts that they occurred to confirm the Word of God:

> Therefore we must give the more earnest heed to the things we have heard, lest we drift away. For if the word spoken through angels proved steadfast, and every transgression and disobedience received a just reward, how shall we escape if we neglect so great a salvation, which at the first began to be spoken by the Lord, and was confirmed to us by those who heard Him, God also bearing witness both with signs and wonders, with various miracles, and gifts of the Holy Spirit, according to His own will? (Hebrews 2:1-4).

Thus, in his gospel account, John noted, "And truly Jesus did many other signs in the presence of His disciples, which are not written in this book; but these are written that you may believe that Jesus is the Christ, the Son of God, and that believing you may have life in His name" (John 20:30-31). To show that miracles were not performed capriciously, we need only to ask a few questions: Why didn't Paul heal his thorn in the flesh (2 Corinthians 12:7-10)? Why didn't Paul heal Timothy's weak stomach (1 Timothy 5:23)? And why didn't Paul heal Trophimus (2 Timothy 4:20)? The answer is that such actions evidently would not have fulfilled the purpose of miracles – to provide confirmation of God's message.

Because miracles served a specific purpose, it follows that if that purpose was fulfilled, there would no longer be a need for the miraculous. Thus, the New Testament suggests that a time would come when miracles would cease to occur. Paul looked forward to that time in his letter to the Ephesians:

> And He Himself gave some to be apostles, some prophets, some evangelists, and some pastors and teachers, for the equipping of the saints for the work of ministry, for the edifying of the body of Christ, till we all come to the unity of the faith and of the knowledge of the Son of God, to a perfect man, to the measure of the stature of the fullness of Christ (4:11-13).

In his first letter to the Corinthians, Paul also described that miracles would cease to occur when the perfect revelation of God was complete:

> Love never fails. But whether there are prophecies, they will fail; whether there are tongues, they will cease; whether there is knowledge, it will vanish away. For we know in part and we prophesy in part. But when that which is perfect has come, then that which is in part will be done away (1 Corinthians 13:8-10).

So what about miracles today? The Bible implies that miracles no longer occur. The duration of the miraculous was limited to the fulfillment of their purpose. What we must remember is that although miracles no longer occur, it does not follow that miracles never occurred. The historical testimony of friends and foes alike still serves to validate the numerous miraculous accounts set forth in Scripture.

## Questions for Consideration

1. What is the identification problem?

2. How can the identification problem be answered?

3. What evidence can be presented in favor of a global flood?

4. Would Noah's ark have been large enough to support every kind of animal? Why or why not?

5. How do we know that dinosaurs and man existed at the same time?

6. Do you think the "behemoth" described in Job 40:15-24 is a dinosaur? Why or why not?

7. What was the purpose of miracles?

8. How would you show from the Bible that miracles no longer occur?

## Chapter 13

# Reason
# and Belief

The importance of belief is stressed throughout Scripture, but nowhere is belief's importance more clearly stated than in Hebrews 11:6: "But without faith it is impossible to please Him, for he who comes to God must believe that He is, and that He is a rewarder of those who diligently seek Him." When we consider the implications of that passage, it becomes quite clear why the study of Christian evidences is so important. This study has sought to set forth evidence for belief in the existence of God, to show why we can trust the Bible, and to look closely at the facts regarding the identity of Jesus. Having concluded that God does exist, that the Bible is the inspired Word of God, and that Jesus is the Son of God, this study will end by concluding that men – who are capable of reasoning about God's existence, the inspiration of the Bible, and the deity of Christ – must use that same rational ability to consider and subsequently obey the plan revealed in Scripture.

## The Appeal to Reason in the New Testament
Although a cursory glance around the religious world might lead one to conclude that reason has very little to do with religious belief, a look at the New Testament will indicate that just the opposite is true. Rather than presenting the gospel in a purely emotional manner, the apostles preached in a way that appealed to the intellect of man. Peter's sermon

on Pentecost serves to illustrate this point. Peter began his sermon by affirming that the events taking place were the fulfillment of the prophecy of Joel (Acts 2:16-21). His appeal to the prophet confirms that his message was based upon more than emotion; instead, he was providing a basis for the conclusion that he eventually drew. Peter went on to affirm that although the Jews could have known the true identity of Jesus by considering the miracles He worked, they rejected the evidence and crucified Him instead (vv. 22-24). He then argued that King David's tomb, a place the Jews would have known, remained filled (v. 29) while the tomb of Jesus was empty (v. 32). And it was only after he had established these three facts (that Joel prophesied about this day, that Jesus' works declared His identity, and that Jesus' tomb was empty) that Peter concluded, "Therefore let all the house of Israel know assuredly that God has made this Jesus, whom you crucified, both Lord and Christ" (v. 36). Far from simply being an emotional plea, Peter's sermon was based upon facts that begged to be considered.

Like Peter, Paul also reasoned with his audiences about Scripture. The following chart serves to illustrate this fact.

## Paul's Use of Reason

| | |
|---|---|
| In Thessalonica ... | "[He] went in to them, and for three Sabbaths reasoned with them from the Scriptures, explaining and demonstrating that Christ had to suffer and rise again from the dead" (Acts 17:2-3). |
| In Athens ... | "he reasoned in the synagogue" (Acts 17:17). |
| In Corinth ... | "he reasoned in the synagogue every Sabbath" (Acts 18:4) |
| In Ephesus ... | "[he] reasoned with the Jews" (Acts 18:19). "And he went into the synagogue and spoke boldly for three months, reasoning and persuading concerning the things of the kingdom of God ... [H]e departed from them and withdrew the disciples, reasoning daily in the school of Tyrannus" (Acts 19:8-9). |

Before Felix ...        "he reasoned about righteousness, self-control, and the judgment to come" (Acts 24:25).

So what possible explanation can be given as to why the apostles sought to reason with those to whom they preached? The only plausible answer is that they did so because they felt that the claims of the gospel were reasonable. To put it another way, they recognized that the evidence sustaining Christianity is capable of supporting the beliefs of rational individuals. Thus, the apostles appealed to the intellect of their listeners and challenged them to obey the gospel out of conviction. If this shows us anything, it shows that the fundamental beliefs of Christianity are tenable. No wonder Paul wrote, "Test all things; hold fast what is good" (1 Thessalonians 5:21). The truth, supported by adequate evidence, awaits those who reason correctly.

## The Implication of the Appeal to Reason

What conclusion should we draw when we realize that the apostles based their preaching upon reason rather than mere emotion? Although many thoughts may come to mind, it seems appropriate to conclude that there must be an objective plan to which men must submit. This plan, by its very nature, must be exclusive. In other words, it is the plan, contained in the Scripture, describing the Savior, who was sent by the God. If this sounds familiar, it is because Jesus asserted something quite similar. Speaking to His apostles, Jesus said, "I am the way, the truth, and the life. No one comes to the Father except through Me" (John 14:6).

It must be noted that not everyone draws this same conclusion. In fact, many people reject the idea that there is an exclusive religion in favor of either inclusivism or pluralism. According to Neil Manson:

> **Inclusivists** agree with exclusivists that the various religions are contrary to one another, but allow that having the right set of religious beliefs is not necessary to salvation. **Pluralists** disagree with both exclusivists and inclusivists. They think it is possible for more than one set of religious truth-claims to be true, and they think salvation can be achieved through a wide variety of religious paths. [Emphasis in original] [1]

Louis Pojman stated many of the questions raised by those who reject exclusivism:

> Is there only one way to God? If God exists, why hasn't he revealed himself in all times and places to all nations and people? Or has he done so, but through different faiths, through different symbols, and different interpretations of himself? Are all religions simply different paths to the same Ultimate Reality?[2]

To answer the charges raised by those who reject the idea of an exclusive religion, one must point to several facts. First, we can know that God exists and that His nature requires Him to deal justly with His creation. Second, we can know, based upon our examination of both internal and external evidences, that the Bible came from God. Thus, the doctrines set forth in the Bible must be viewed as authoritative. Third, we can know that Jesus is who He claimed to be – the Son of God. So when Jesus speaks, He speaks the truth.

So what does this mean? It means that Christianity not only makes exclusive claims but that it is the exclusive religion. That, of course, is why Jesus charged His followers with the responsibility of evangelizing the world: "Go into all the world and preach the gospel to every creature. He who believes and is baptized will be saved; but he who does not believe will be condemned" (Mark 16:15-16). This command was taken quite seriously by the first-century Christians. In fact, by as early as A.D. 62, Paul described the success of the Christians in this regard:

> And you, who once were alienated and enemies in your mind by wicked works, yet now He has reconciled in the body of His flesh through death, to present you holy, and blameless, and above reproach in His sight – if indeed you continue in the faith, grounded and steadfast, and are not moved away from the hope of the gospel which you heard, which was preached to every creature under heaven, of which I, Paul, became a minister (Colossians 1:21-23).

If the Bible is correct, as has been established in this work, there is only one plan of salvation. That is why Peter declared, "Nor is there salvation in any other, for there is no other name under heaven given among men by which we must be saved" (Acts 4:12).

## The Gospel Is Reasonable

With the exclusive nature of Christianity upheld, we must now turn our attention to the gospel plan itself. What is it that makes the gospel plan reasonable? And why did Paul argue to the Thessalonians "that the Christ had to suffer and rise again from the dead" (Acts 17:3)? The answer to these questions lies in the very reason for Jesus' sacrifice – He died to pay the price for man's sins. Such a sacrifice was necessary because of the terrible nature of sin (see Isaiah 59:1-2). Because God is just, He could not let sin go unpunished (see Hebrews 2:1-4). And because His love for humanity demanded that He make provisions for the redemption of mankind (see 1 Timothy 2:4), God sent His perfect Son to die vicariously for the world. Paul described this act in 2 Corinthians 5:21: "For He made Him who knew no sin to be sin for us, that we might become the righteousness of God in Him." Thus, doing what animal sacrifices could never do (Hebrews 10:4), Jesus died so that the sins of man could be forgiven (Ephesians 1:7).

Just because Jesus died, we ought not to conclude that all men will benefit from His death. The sad reality is that most will not. Noting this Himself, Jesus said, "Enter by the narrow gate; for wide is the gate and broad is the way that leads to destruction, and there are many who go in by it. Because narrow is the gate and difficult is the way which leads to life, and there are few who find it" (Matthew 7:13-14). When we realize that God's plan of salvation is available to all men (Titus 2:11), the only conclusion we can draw is that those who are lost must have failed to obey Jesus. After all, Jesus is "the author of eternal salvation to all who obey Him" (Hebrews 5:9).

So what must one do to be saved? When we examine that question as it is asked in Scripture, we find three distinctive passages. The first passage is within the context of Peter's sermon on Pentecost. After being charged with the crime of crucifying the Son of God, the Jews responded in a noble way. Luke wrote, "Now when they heard this, they were cut to the heart, and said to Peter and the rest of the apostles, 'Men and brethren, what shall we do?' " (Acts 2:37).[3] Peter answered, "Repent, and let every one of you be baptized in the name of Jesus Christ for the remission of sins; and you shall receive the gift of the Holy Spirit" (v. 38). Although one might find it curious that Peter said nothing about belief as he answered the Jews' question regarding salvation, it must be remembered that these individuals already believed in God – they were in Jerusalem to observe Pentecost. Additionally, their response to Peter's sermon indicates that they accepted His conclusion that they were guilty of killing the Son of God.

A second occasion in which an individual asks about salvation is found in Acts 9:1-19 where we read about the journey of Saul of Tarsus toward Damascus:

> As he journeyed he came near Damascus, and suddenly a light shone around him from heaven. Then he fell to the ground, and heard a voice saying to him, "Saul, Saul, why are you persecuting Me?" And he said, "Who are You, Lord?" Then the Lord said, "I am Jesus, whom you are persecuting. It is hard for you to kick against the goads." So he, trembling and astonished, said, "Lord, what do You want me to do?" Then the Lord said to him, "Arise and go into the city, and you will be told what you must do" (vv. 3-6).

Upon arriving in that city, the text reveals that Saul was fasting and praying (Acts 9:9, 11) – actions that seem, within the context, to be associated with repentance. Thus, when Ananias arrived to tell Saul what to do, he simply said, "And now why are you waiting? Arise and be baptized, and wash away your sins, calling on the name of the Lord" (22:16). Because Saul had seen the Lord, he did not need to be told to believe; because he was fasting and praying, he did not need to be told to repent. Instead, he needed to be baptized.

In Acts 16:30, we find the third occasion when an individual asks the question, "What must I do to be saved?" On this occasion, the individual who asked the question, known as the Philippian jailer, was a Gentile. Unlike the individuals who heard Peter preach on Pentecost or Saul of Tarsus, he had little if any knowledge regarding the one true God. Thus, Paul and Silas answered the question by declaring where the jailer needed to start. They said, "Believe on the Lord Jesus Christ, and you will be saved, you and your household" (v. 31). To conclude that this was all that Paul and Silas told the Philippian jailer would be a mistake. In fact, the text reveals that "they spoke the word of the Lord to him and to all who were in his house" (v. 32). After hearing this message, the jailer "washed their stripes" – an act of repentance – and was baptized (v. 33).

In all three passages, we find the following components: the individuals heard the gospel plan, they believed, they repented, they publicly recognized Jesus, and they were baptized. Because of these actions, it is reasonable to conclude that those who would be saved today must do no less.

## Reasons to Believe

We began this book by asking, "Why study Christian evidences?" We end it by asserting that the evidence that supports Christianity gives us ample reasons to believe. It is my hope that all those who read this book will not only be given a reason to believe in God, to trust His word, and to follow His Son but that they will also be better prepared to face the challenges that attack their faith.

## Questions for Consideration

1. How would you describe the preaching of Peter and Paul?

2. What three sections of Peter's sermon appealed to the reason of those present on Pentecost?

3. What conclusion can we draw from the apostle's appeal to reason?

4. What does it mean for a religion to be exclusive?

5. What is meant by the terms "inclusivism" and "pluralism"?

6. Which of the following terms best describes your view of Christianity: exclusivism, inclusivism or pluralism? Why?

7. Why did Jesus have to come to the earth and die?

8. What must man do to be saved?

# Selected Bibliography

Anselm. *Anselm of Canterbury: The Major Works*. Oxford: Oxford UP, 1998.

Augustine. *City of God*. *Nicene and Post-Nicene Fathers*. Ed. Philip Schaff. Vol. 2. Peabody: Hendrickson Publishers, 1994.

---. *Confessions*. *Nicene and Post-Nicene Fathers*. Ed. Philip Schaff. Vol. 1. Peabody: Hendrickson, 1994.

Bales, James D. and Woolsey Teller. *Bales-Teller Debate*. Shreveport: Lambert, 1976.

Baxter, Batsell Barrett. *I Believe Because ...* . Grand Rapids: Baker, 1971.

Bretall, Robert, ed. *A Kierkegaard Anthology*. New York: Modern Library, 1946.

Bromling, Brad T. *Be Sure: A Study in Christian Evidences*. Montgomery: Apologetics, 1995.

Butt, Kyle and Eric Lyons. *Truth Be Told: Exposing the Myth of Evolution*. Montgomery: Apologetics, 2005.

Campbell, Alexander and Robert Owen. *Campbell-Owen Debate*. Nashville: McQuiddy, 1957.

Clarke, Adam. *Clarke's Commentary*. Vol. 5. New York: Abingdon, reprinted, n.d.

Copleston, Frederick. *A History of Philosophy*. Vol. 1. New York: Doubleday, 1993.

Craig, Clarence Tucker. *The Beginning of Christianity.* New York: Abingdon, 1943.

Dehoff, George W. *Why We Believe the Bible.* Murfreesboro: Dehoff, 1956.

Hales, Steven and Scott Lowe, eds. *Delight in Thinking.* New York: McGraw-Hill, 2007.

Harrub, Brad and Bert Thompson. *The Truth About Human Origins.* Montgomery: Apologetics, 2003.

Hick, John, ed. *The Existence of God.* New York: Macmillian, 1978.

---. *Evil and the God of Love.* San Francisco: Harper & Row, 1977.

Hodge, Charles. *Systematic Theology.* Vol. 1. Peabody, MA: Hendrickson, reprinted, n.d.

Jackson, Wayne. *Bible Words and Theological Terms Made Easy.* Stockton: Courier, 2002.

---. *Fortify Your Faith.* Montgomery: Apologetics, 1974.

---. "Jesus and History." *Think* May 2006: 9.

---. "The Pre-Existence and Birth of Jesus." *The Spiritual Sword* April 1970: 3.

Josephus. *The Works of Josephus.* Trans. William Whiston. Peabody: Hendrickson, 2003.x

Kebric, Robert B. *Roman People.* Mountain View: Mayfield, 1993.

Leupold, H.C. *Exposition of Genesis.* Vol. 1. Grand Rapids: Baker, 1958.

Lewis, C.S. *Mere Christianity.* New York: Touchstone, 1996.

---. *The Problem of Pain.* New York: Macmillan, 1978.

Lyons, Eric. *The Anvil Rings.* Vol. 1. Montgomery: Apologetics, 2003.

Martin, Raymond and Christopher Bernard, eds. *God Matters: Readings in the Philosophy of Religion.* New York: Longman, 2003.

Mattox, F.W. *The Eternal Kingdom.* Delight: Gospel Light, 1961.

McDowell, Josh. *Evidence that Demands a Verdict.* Vol. 1. Nashville: Thomas Nelson, 1979.

McGarvey, J.W. *Evidences of Christianity.* Indianapolis: Faith and Facts, n.d.

Miller, Ed L. *Questions That Matter.* Boston: McGraw-Hill, 1998.

Monser, J.W., ed. *An Encyclopedia on the Evidences.* Nashville: Gospel Advocate, 1961.

Morison, Frank. *Who Moved the Stone?* Grand Rapids: Zondervan, 2002.

Mosher, Sr., Keith A. *The Book God "Breathed."* Published Privately, n.d.

Nash, Ronald H. *The Concept of God.* Grand Rapids: Zondervan, 1983

Orr, James, ed. *International Standard Bible Encyclopedia.* 1929. Vol. 3. USA: Peabody, MA, 2002.

Owen, H.P. *The Moral Argument for Christian Theism.* London: George Allen and Unwin, 1965.

Petit, Francois. *The Problem of Evil.* New York: Hawthorn, 1959.

Pojman, Louis P. *Philosophy of Religion: An Anthology.* Belmont: Wadsworth, 1998.

Rimmer, Harry. *The Harmony of Science and Scripture.* Grand Rapids: Eerdmans, 1970.

Rowe, William L. *Philosophy of Religion.* Belmont: Wadsworth, 2001.

Sanders, Phil. "Who Is This Jesus?" *Think* May 2006: 6.

Schaff, Philip. *History of the Christian Church.* Vol. 1. Grand Rapids: Eerdmans, 1966.

Sears, Jack Wood. *Conflict and Harmony in Science and the Bible.* Grand Rapids: Baker, 1969.

Smith, Wilbur M. *Therefore Stand.* Grand Rapids: Baker, 1968.

Trench, R.C. *Notes on the Miracles of Our Lord.* Grand Rapids: Baker, 1958.

Trice, Allison N. and Charles H. Roberson. *Bible vs. Modernism.* Nashville: Gospel Advocate, 1946.

Vincent, Marvin R. *Vincent's Word Studies in the New Testament.* Vol. 4. Peabody: Hendrickson, n.d.

Warfield, B.B. *The Plan of Salvation.* Grand Rapids: Eerdmans, 1977.

Warren, Thomas B. *Our Loving God – A Sun and Shield.* Moore: National Christian, 1998.

---. *Sin, Suffering – and God.* Jonesboro: National Christian, 1980.

---, ed. *The Spiritual Sword,* April 1971.

Warren, Thomas B. and Antony Flew. *The Warren-Flew Debate.* Moore: National Christian, 1977.

Winkler, Wendell, ed. *Difficult Texts of the Old Testament Explained.* Montgomery: Winkler, 1982.

---, ed. *The Holy Scriptures.* Montgomery: Winkler, 1979.

# Endnotes

## Chapter 1

[1]Søren Kierkegaard, *Concluding Unscientific Postscript to the "Philosophical Fragments,"* *A Kierkegaard Anthology*, ed. Robert Bretall (New York: The Modern Library, 1946) 215.

## Chapter 2

[1]Nathan Segars, "God's Existence – Causal Arguments," *2004 Freed-Hardeman University Lectures*, ed. David Lipe (Henderson: Freed-Hardeman University, 2004) 379.

[2]Thomas Aquinas, "The Five Ways," *The Existence of God*, ed. John Hick (New York: Macmillian Publishing, 1978) 82.

[3]Aquinas 83-84.

[4]James D. Bales, *Bales-Teller Debate* (Shreveport: Lambert Book House, 1976) 23-24.

[5]Bales 23-24.

[6]Aquinas 83-84.

## Chapter 3

[1]Anselm of Canterbury, *Proslogion*, *Anselm of Canterbury: The Major Works* (Oxford: Oxford UP, 1998), 87.

[2]Anselm of Canterbury 87-88.

[3]William L. Rowe, *Philosophy of Religion* (Belmont: Wadsworth, 2001) 34.

[4]Rowe 35.

[5]H.P. Owen, *The Moral Argument for Christian Theism* (London: George Allen and Unwin, 1965) 17.

[6]Hastings Rashdall, "The Moral Argument," *The Existence of God*, ed. John Hick (New York: Macmillan, 1964) 149-50.

[7]C.S. Lewis, *Mere Christianity* (New York: Touchstone, 1996) 18.

[8]Owen 19.

[9]Lewis 29.

[10]Lewis 25.

[11]Thomas B. Warren, *The Warren-Flew Debate* (Moore: National Christian Press, 1977) 173.

## Chapter 4

[1]A.E. Taylor, "The Vindication of Religion," *The Existence of God*, ed. John Hick (New York: Macmillan, 1964) 154-55.

[2]Taylor 155.

[3]Taylor 153.

[4]J.W. McGarvey, *Evidences of Christianity*, Part 2 (Indianapolis: Faith and Facts Press, n.d.) 116.

[5]McGarvey 117-118.

[6]Frank Morison, *Who Moved the Stone?* (Grand Rapids: Zondervan, 2002) 176.

[7]Alexander Campbell, *Campbell-Owen Debate* (Nashville: McQuiddy, 1957) 91.

## Chapter 5

[1]Frederick Copleston, *A History of Philosophy*, Vol. 1 (New York: Doubleday, 1993) 405.

[2]John Hick, *Evil and the God of Love* (San Francisco: Harper & Row, 1977) 5.

[3]Hick 5.

[4]Francois Petit, *The Problem of Evil* (New York: Hawthorn Books, 1959) 11.

[5]William L. Rowe, *Philosophy of Religion: An Introduction* (Belmont: Wadsworth, 2001) 93.

[6]Ed L. Miller, *Questions That Matter* (Boston: McGraw-Hill, 1998) 307.

[7]Gottfried Leibniz, from *Theodicy*, quoted in *God Matters: Readings in the Philosophy of Religion*, ed. Raymond Martin and Christopher Bernard (New York: Longman, 2003) 278.

[8]Hick 168.

[9]Hick 168.

[10]C.S. Lewis, *The Problem of Pain* (New York: Macmillan Publishing, 1978) 93.

[11]Lewis 28.

[12]Thomas B. Warren, *Sin, Suffering – and God* (Jonesboro: National Christian, 1980) 301.

[13]Warren, *Sin* 304-05.

[14]Augustine, *City of God* (11.9).

[15]Thomas B. Warren, *Our Loving God – A Sun and Shield* (Moore: National Christian, 1998) 55.

## Chapter 6

[1]William L. Rowe, *Philosophy of Religion: An Introduction* (Belmont: Wadsworth, 2001) 14.

[2]Rowe 150.

[3]Ronald H. Nash, *The Concept of God* (Grand Rapids: Zondervan, 1983) 57.

[4]Adam Clarke, *Clarke's Commentary*, Vol. 5 (New York: Abingdon, reprinted, n.d.) 702.

[5]Rowe 150.

[6]Rowe 158.

[7]Charles Hodge, *Systematic Theology*, Vol. 1 (Peabody, MA: Hendrickson Publishers, reprinted, n.d.) 401.

[8]B.B. Warfield, *The Plan of Salvation* (Grand Rapids: Eerdmans, 1977) 71-72.

[9]Hodge 878.

## Chapter 7

[1]The term "Scripture" is used in reference to the Old Testament in Luke 24:27. It is also used to refer to the words of Jesus in 1 Timothy 5:17 (cf. Luke 10:7) and to refer to the words of Paul in 2 Peter 3:15-16.

[2]Marvin R. Vincent, *Vincent's Word Studies in the New Testament*, Vol. 4 (Peabody: Hendrickson, n.d.) 317.

[3]Wayne Jackson, *Bible Words and Theological Terms Made Easy* (Stockton: Courier, 2002) 88.

[4]Keith A. Mosher Sr., *The Book God "Breathed"* (Published Privately) 16-17.

[5]Wayne Jackson, *Fortify Your Faith* (Montgomery: Apologetics, 1974) 52-53.

[6]George W. Dehoff, *Why We Believe the Bible* (Murfreesboro: Dehoff, 1956) 70.

[7]Alexander Campbell, *Campbell-Owen Debate* (Nashville: McQuiddy, 1957) 351.

[8]Batsell Barrett Baxter, *I Believe Because ...* (Grand Rapids: Baker, 1971) 186.

[9]Dehoff 70.

## Chapter 8

[1]Wayne Jackson, *Fortify Your Faith* (Montgomery: Apologetics, 1974) 63.

[2]George W. Dehoff, *Why We Believe the Bible* (Murfreesboro: Dehoff, 1956) 47-48.

[3]Batsell Barrett Baxter, *I Believe Because ...* (Grand Rapids: Baker, 1971) 196.

[4]Jackson 63-64. Used with permission.

[5]Allison N. Trice and Charles H. Roberson, *Bible vs. Modernism* (Nashville: Gospel Advocate, 1946) 137-38.

[6]Bill J. Humble, "External Evidences for the Bible's Inspiration – Archaeology," *The Holy Scriptures*, ed. Wendell Winkler (Montgomery: Winkler, 1979) 93.

[7]James Orr, ed., *International Standard Bible Encyclopedia*, 1929, Vol. 3 (Peabody, MA: Hendrickson Publishing, 2002) 1402F.

[8]Humble 97.

[9]Eric Lyons, *The Anvil Rings*, Vol. 1 (Montgomery: Apologetics, 2003) 99.

[10]Lyons 99.

[11]For a further study of this point, see Keith Mosher Sr., *The Book God "Breathed"* (Published Privately) 98-106.

[12]Mosher 106.

[13]J.W. McGarvey, *Evidences of Christianity*, Part 2 (Indianapolis: Faith and Facts, n.d.) 218.

[14]McGarvey 222.

## Chapter 9

[1]Josephus, *The Antiquities of the Jews* (18.3.3), *The Works of Josephus*, Trans. William Whiston (Peabody: Hendrickson, 2003) 480.

[2]Clarence Tucker Craig, *The Beginning of Christianity* (New York: Abingdon, 1943) 57.

[3]The passage is quoted by Eusebius in his *Ecclesiastical History* (1.11). This book was written no later than A.D. 326.

[4]Josephus 538.

[5]Tacitus, Annals (XV.44), quoted in *Evidence That Demands a Verdict*, Vol. 1, Josh McDowell (Nashville, Thomas Nelson, 1979) 81-82.

[6]F.W. Mattox, *The Eternal Kingdom* (Delight: Gospel Light, 1961) 34.

[7]Robert B. Kebric, *Roman People* (Mountain View: Mayfield, 1993) 211-12.

[8]Wayne Jackson, "Jesus and History," *Think*, May 2006, 9.

[9]*The World Book Encyclopedia Dictionary*, Vol. 1 (Chicago: Doubleday, 1963) 81.

[10]Philip Schaff, *History of the Christian Church*, Vol. 1 (Grand Rapids: Eerdmans, 1966) 478.

[11]Phil Sanders, "Who Is This Jesus?" *Think*, May 2006, 6. Used with permission.

## Chapter 10

[1]Eric Lyons and Kyle Butt, "The Very Works That I Do Bear Witness of Me," *Reason and Revelation*, March 2006, 20.

[2]R.C. Trench, *Notes on the Miracles of Our Lord* (Grand Rapids: Baker, 1958) 58-59.

[3]Wayne Jackson, "The Pre-Existence and Birth of Jesus," *The Spiritual Sword*, April 1970, 3.

[4]Jackson 3

[5]For a detailed defense of Jesus' resurrection, the reader is encouraged to take a closer look at chapter 4 of this book.

[6]Philip Schaff, *The Person of Christ* (Boston: American Tract Society, 1882) 32-33, quoted in *I Believe Because* ..., Batsell Barrett Baxter (Grand Rapids: Baker Book House, 1971) 218.

[7]Schaff 29-30, Baxter 219.

[8]Bernard Ramm, *Protestant Christian Evidences* (Chicago: Moody Press, 1933) 170, quoted in *I Believe Because* ..., Batsell Barrett Baxter (Grand Rapids: Baker Book House, 1971) 219.

[9]This does not mean that validity is solely based upon the number of individuals who believe a particular thing. For example, many believe that Muhammad was a prophet of God. What this does mean, however, is that one must take into consideration why a large number of individuals believe a particular fact. Do their reasons stand up to criticism? Or do they falter when put to the test?

[10]C.S. Lewis, *Mere Christianity* (New York: Touchstone, 1996) 56.

## Chapter 11

[1]Wilbur M. Smith, *Therefore Stand* (Grand Rapids: Baker, 1968) 272.

[2]Smith 273.

[3]Henry M. Morris, *Studies in the Bible and Science* (Grand Rapids: Baker Book House, 1966) 49-50, quoted in *I Believe Because* ..., Batsell Barrett Baxter (Grand Rapids: Baker Book House, 1971) 127-128.

[4]James D. Bales, "The Theory of Evolution: A Philosophic Problem," *The Spiritual Sword*, April 1971, 1-2.

[5]Theodosius Dobzhasky, *Genetics and the Origin of Species* (New York: Columbia UP, 1951) 11, quoted by Bales 2.

[6]G.A. Kerkut, *Implications of Evolution* (Oxford: Pergamon Press, 1965) 6, quoted in *Conflict and Harmony in Science and the Bible*, Jack Wood Sears (Grand Rapids: Baker Book House, 1969) 33.

[7]Frederick Copleston, *A History of Philosophy*, Vol. 1 (New York: Image, 1993) 25.

[8]Copleston 25.

[9]Neil A. Manson, "The Design Argument," *Delight in Thinking*, ed. Steven Hales and Scott Lowe (New York: McGraw-Hill, 2007) 181.

[10]Manson 181.

[11]Oliver Lodge, *Man and the Universe* (London: 1909) 19, 29, quoted in Smith 274-75.

[12]Austin H. Clark, *The New Evolution, Zoogenesis* (Baltimore: Williams and

Wilkins, 1930) 129ff, quoted in Baxter 139-40.

[13]Brad Harrub and Bert Thompson, *The Truth About Human Origins* (Montgomery: Apologetics, 2003) 12.

[14]Harrub and Thompson 84.

[15]Richard Holt Hutton, *Essays*, Vol. 1, 64, quoted in *An Encyclopedia on the Evidences*, J. W. Monser (Nashville: Gospel Advocate, 1961) 291-92.

[16]Wayne Jackson, *Fortify Your Faith* (Montgomery: Apologetics, 1974) 38-39.

[17]Smith 309-10.

[18]Smith 329.

[19]Foy L. Kirkpatrick, "The Creationist and the Time Problem," *The Spiritual Sword*, April 1971, 39.

[20]In his debate with Antony Flew, Thomas B. Warren asserted that in order for evolution to be proven true, evolutionists must show that matter is eternal; life came from rocks and dirt; consciousness came from that which had no consciousness; conscience resulted from that which had no conscience; intelligence came from that which had no intelligence; and human beings came from that which was not human. Warren fittingly described this task as "Flew's Prison." Thomas B. Warren and Antony Flew, *The Warren Flew Debate* (Moore: National Christian Press, 1977) 8.

[21]Augustine, *Confessions* (10.6.9).

## Chapter 12

[1]Neil A. Manson, "The Cosmological Argument," (Unpublished class notes, 2005).

[2]For a detailed examination of the attributes of God, see chapter 6 of this book.

[3]H.C. Leupold, *Exposition of Genesis*, Vol. 1 (Grand Rapids: Baker, 1958) 302.

[4]Harry Rimmer, *The Harmony of Science and Scripture* (Grand Rapids: Wm. B. Eerdmans, 1970).

[5]D.R. Dungan, *Modern Phases of Scepticism*, 217-18, quoted in *An Encyclopedia on the Evidences*, J.W. Monser (Nashville: Gospel Advocate, 1961) 332.

[6]Warren Wilcox, "Difficult Texts From Genesis," *Difficult Texts of the Old Testament Explained*, ed. Wendell Winkler (Montgomery: Winkler Publications, 1982) 221.

[7]The ancient historian, Herodotus (c. 480-425 B.C.), wrote, "The winged snakes resemble watersnakes; their wings are not feathered, but are like a bat's." quoted in Herodotus, *The Histories* (Middlesex, England: Penguin Books, 1975) 158.

[8]Brad T. Bromling, *Be Sure: A Study in Christian Evidences* (Montgomery: Apologetics, 1995) 73.

[9]Kyle Butt and Eric Lyons, *Truth Be Told: Exposing the Myth of Evolution* (Montgomery: Apologetics, 2005) 128.

## Chapter 13

[1]Neil A. Manson, "Religious Diversity," (Unpublished class notes, 2005)

[2]Louis P. Pojman, *Philosophy of Religion: An Anthology* (Belmont: Wadsworth, 1998) 507.

[3]It is significant that Peter had previously told these individuals: "And it shall come to pass that whoever calls on the name of the Lord shall be saved" (Acts 2:21). Thus, we may conclude that they understood that the act of calling on the name of the Lord meant more than merely crying out, "Lord, save us." For this reason, they turned to Peter for further explanation which he gladly offered.

CPSIA information can be obtained
at www.ICGtesting.com
Printed in the USA
JSHW021328130920
7673JS00006B/100